D1495067

20 Vintage 11

Sketching
and Drawing

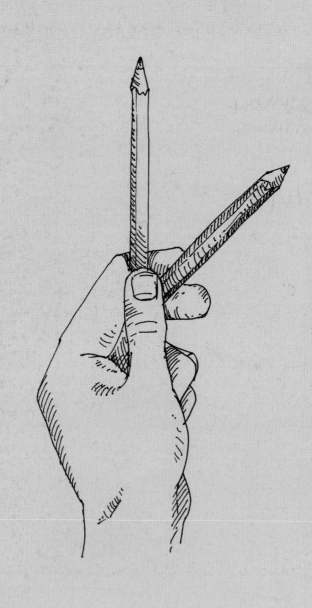

Sketching and Drawing

Matt Pagett

APPLE

First published in the UK in 2011 by
Apple Press
7 Greenland Street
London NW1 0ND

www.apple-press.com

ISBN: 978-1-84543-399-4

Conceived, designed and produced by
Quid Publishing
Level 4, Sheridan House
114 Western Road
Hove BN3 1DD
England

Design by Lindsey Johns

Printed in China by 1010 Printing International Ltd.

10 9 8 7 6 5 4 3 2 1

Contents

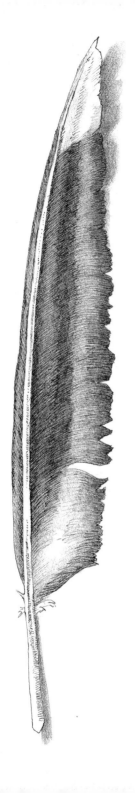

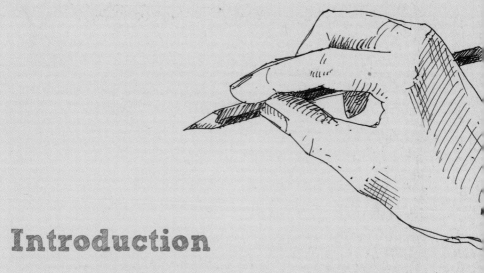

Introduction

The artistic impulse is felt universally, and usually first takes form,

joyously, in early childhood. Splodges and lines articulate the imagination;

our inner world takes a trip outside. In later years, that urge to create often

gets lost in the mist, buried among insecurities and other commitments,

and art becomes something we did, rather than something we do. These

books aim to guide you back into the realm of artistic creation and

expression, encouraging awareness of and confidence in your own

individual abilities and talent. Consider the skills and drills contained

within these pages as the building blocks for future growth as you develop a

personal and distinct style. And with practice, your own version of what

'perfect' means will emerge and blossom.

Welcome

Drawing is one of the most fundamental urges. As part of a collective desire to communicate, play or express ourselves, we draw before we learn to write. Regardless of ability, we have all tried it and most probably still do it to some extent. Were you doodling the last time someone on the other end of the phone put you on hold? Did you scribble a quick map to show a friend how to get from A to B? What about the marks you made with that old ballpoint pen to check that it was still working? Swiss artist Paul Klee famously said, 'A drawing is simply taking a line for a walk'. In this context, most of us can already consider ourselves as people who draw.

Seeing and Drawing

There are, of course, more levels of drawing to both practise and appreciate. A drawing can be a compelling piece of art in its own right, full of intricacy and sensitivity. Equally, drawing underpins most of the other visual arts, such as painting, sculpture and printmaking. It has been important to humankind since prehistory, and is not just limited to the West. By learning more about drawing, we mine a rich cultural seam that runs through all of us.

A drawing can be simple, complex, beautiful, ugly, informative, expressive – indeed, any of these and more. It is always rooted in vision, and allows us to record how we see our surroundings. In turn, by choosing to draw something in front of us – be it an old jug, a favourite aunt or a view across rocks and waves to some foggy, far-flung peninsula – it helps us to see, and see, and see again. In our waking lives, our eyes are always 'on', constantly receiving and processing visual information. When we draw, we edit out and focus on just one particular bit. Things slow down and we become active participants in the world around us.

Drawing is a language in which letters, words and sentences have been replaced by

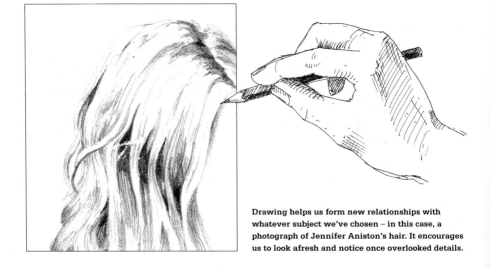

Drawing helps us form new relationships with whatever subject we've chosen – in this case, a photograph of Jennifer Aniston's hair. It encourages us to look afresh and notice once overlooked details.

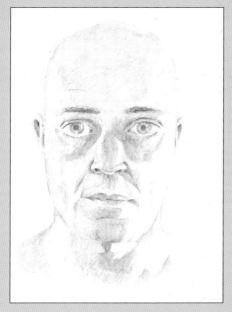
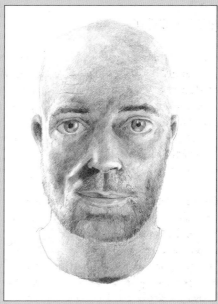

Over time, the more you draw, the more you will learn to see. The self-portrait here on the left was made about seven years before the one on the right. It is actually the same drawing reworked at a later date. Notice how the more recent image contains a lot more information and confidence; an improvement that only comes with practice.

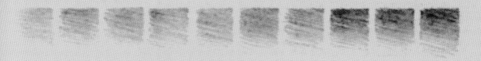

form, tone and texture. Just as language is learned, so too the basic skills of drawing can be studied and understood. By picking up this book you've made a start. You'll learn about the materials and techniques that have evolved over centuries to become integral to the drawing process. You'll learn about the importance of looking and of practising. You'll be encouraged to find things out for yourself in addition to following the exercises given.

Hopefully, after you've read the last page, you'll have the skills and confidence to take your own individual lines for a walk, on journeys that will continue to inspire, surprise and delight you.

CAN DRAW!

This book is a mini-manifesto for personal improvement and artistic growth. It doesn't subscribe to the oft-quoted statement 'I can't draw.' That's like saying 'I can't drive/cook/speak French.' No one is born driving, cooking or speaking French: they are skills that are learned. What is important is that you want to learn. By wanting to learn, you keep up the essential motivation and focus that helps transform the pain and frustration of ignorance into the pleasure of understanding.

Using This Book

Maybe you haven't drawn since school, or maybe you're feeling a bit rusty after a few years' hiatus. The aim here is to ease you, ever so gently, back into the warm pool of artistic production. Don't be alarmed by any of the exercises, no matter how scary they may appear at first. Stick with it, and above all, keep practising.

As its title suggests, this book focuses on the very basics of drawing practice. After a brief introduction, including a quick skate through thousands of years of artistic production, it turns to the different drawing tools and materials that are available. Following a discussion of a few basic things to consider before starting a picture, the next section provides a number of 'loosening-up' exercises useful to anyone, newcomer or old pro.

The book then takes a look at some of the essential areas of drawing (namely, composition, line, value and surface). The breadth of each area is sufficiently wide to go into more detailed analysis, and exercises along the way encourage you to try each area out for yourself. Each section concludes with a larger project that focuses on what's been discussed. Finally, ideas on developing your own skills and language are followed by a few tips and hints as well as a glossary.

Feel free to use the photographs provided as a starting point for your exercises, although you may find it more rewarding to select your own subjects. And while you may like to dip in and out, the book is probably best followed chronologically (certainly, the first time around), as that's how it has been designed.

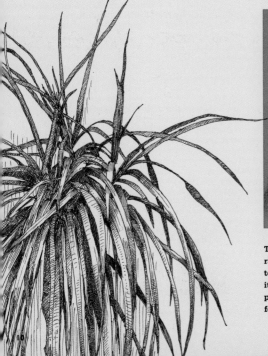

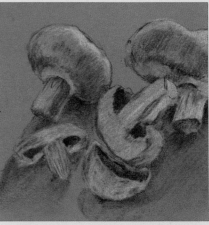

The examples given in the following pages range from tight, densely packed pen drawings to much softer, looser pastels. Each medium has its own unique characteristics, and it's only by playing around that you'll discover what works for you.

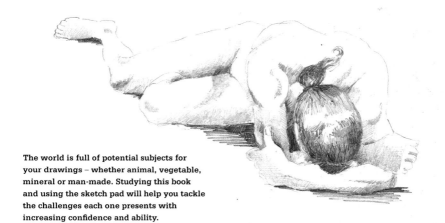

The world is full of potential subjects for your drawings – whether animal, vegetable, mineral or man-made. Studying this book and using the sketch pad will help you tackle the challenges each one presents with increasing confidence and ability.

Using Your Sketch Pad

The exercises are designed so that you can easily try them out and practise them using the sketch pad that accompanies this book. They are mostly quick and easy to set up, and the folder should make sure that everything stays in place. Of course you can use other paper, too, and when working on larger projects, you may want to invest in some bigger paper to give yourself more room to manoeuvre.

Try These

You'll notice throughout the book that there are various 'Try This' exercises. These are short, playful mini-exercises that either introduce or complement the larger topics being discussed. Some will be easily completed in the sketch pad, while others encourage you to think about each topic in a new or different way. Each 'Try This' exercise, much like the rest of the book, aims to broaden your understanding of what drawing is, what it can be and what it involves. You'll soon start to think about the issues they raise and, in doing so, discover and develop your own individual strengths.

Basic Materials

A suggested list of what to buy before you start walking your line:

- 4 pencils of different grades (hard to soft, for example, H, HB, 2B, 5B)
- 1 pack of charcoal sticks (various widths)
- 2 fibre-tip pens (thick and thin tips)
- 1 pack of pastels (chalk or oil)
- 1 pack of water-soluble coloured pencils
- 1 sharpener
- 1 plastic rubber
- 1 putty rubber
- 1 can of fixative spray

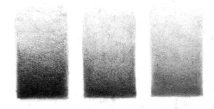

What Is Drawing?

It's useful to consider the various ways you might approach your drawings and how they can be interpreted. Understanding your process and what your drawing means to you creates a sensibility that will filter through to both your drawing and to your viewer.

Definition

According to the *New Oxford American Dictionary*, a drawing is 'a picture or diagram made with a pencil, pen or crayon rather than paint, esp. one drawn in monochrome'. For all its supposed authority, one can't help feeling slightly shortchanged by this definition. Paint can certainly be used to draw with, and the wide range of coloured drawing materials available these days calls into question the emphasis on 'monochrome'. That said, it is a useful starting point. Perhaps we could add that a drawing conveys ideas and information through a series of marks and strokes put down on any suitable flat surface. It is also a vehicle for self-expression, and a means of communication.

Each drawing bears witness to the mutual relationship between artist and subject. If either moves, the drawing changes. It is like an extended photograph, a snapshot stretched over time to communicate what something looked like from a particular viewpoint. Furthermore, because the artist has left evidence of his own hand and eye at work, we can sometimes detect a sense of his feelings or state of mind as the drawing was made. Turning that reflection back on ourselves, each drawing represents a connection between artist and audience, a conversation.

Your Drawing and You

It's not easy to simplify the whys and wherefores of artistic production. Art, like life, can be full of contradictions, but by thinking about the different reasons and methods for making and reading drawings, you can gain a richer understanding of your own work.

Approach A picture can be drawn with a minimum of fuss – clean lines, tidy shading, precise angles – a descriptive and objective account of how the subject appears. On the other hand, a drawing can also be full of expressive marks, scribbled areas that have been worked, then reworked – a subjective picture that conveys as much about the artist as it does about the subject. Do you want to record or do you want to express? Or do you want to do both?

Intention Drawings are made for any number of reasons, and the final destination can have a big impact on the process you adopt. Do you want to capture a fleeting moment of visual interest (in which case a quick sketch in any medium on a scrap of paper will do)? Is the drawing to be a rough study for something more involved? Or do you want to indulge yourself and spend a few hours with your subject, leading to a piece of work that stands on its own?

Method Given the wealth of materials to choose from, before you start, consider which kinds you want to use. Over time you'll develop personal preferences for a particular medium or implement, though don't let that stop you from experimenting with new ones. Forcing yourself out of your comfort zone can keep things exciting and help you develop.

What is important to remember is that there is no right or wrong way to go about it. Each approach, intention and method has its own benefits and pitfalls – the key lies in understanding them and learning from them.

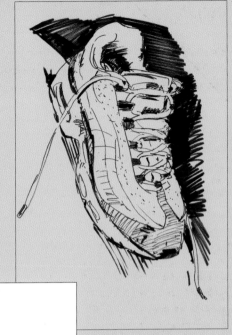

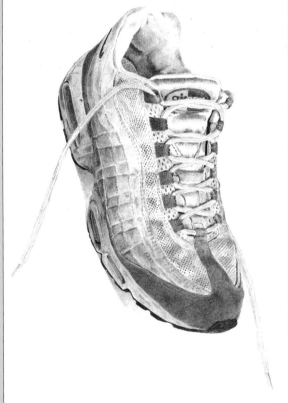

The same trainer at the same angle, but two very different drawings. The pen drawing above is more fluid, energetic and expressive. The pencil drawing on the left is cooler, more objective and detached, and more closely resembles a photograph. The pencil version took longer, and made me look a lot harder at what was in front of me, while the pen drawing felt more playful. Both have their own stories to tell and their own personality. Which do you prefer? There's no right or wrong answer, just your own personal preference.

Looking at Drawing 1

As previously mentioned, drawing is a pursuit that dates back millennia. Whatever your ability, when you draw, you connect with a glorious tradition. Your skill level and confidence may not yet be up there with the greats, but by looking at their work, you can get an idea of what that long history looks like, and take inspiration accordingly. The pictures featured here offer you the tiniest taste of what's yours for the taking. Do some research yourself, online or in local galleries or museums, and find out more.

1 | **Cave painting, Lascaux, France, c. 15000 B.C.E.:** Famous as prime examples of Upper Paleolithic art, this series of cave drawings was discovered in 1940. Large animals, humans and abstract symbols adorn a series of cave chambers, and were daubed directly onto the walls with mineral pigments. Whether the images had a ceremonial significance, or if they were drawn as a means of communication, no one can tell. Here, the simple elegance of the animal plays with the surrounding abstract symbols and expresses a sophistication not normally associated with early humankind.

2 | **Dürer, *Praying Hands*, 1508:** German artist Dürer was an outstanding draughtsman. His observations are so rich and so acute that even a simple pair of hands, perhaps drawn as a study for a larger work, hints at a much more complex story: Whose hands are these? Why are they praying? They appear to loom out of the coloured ground, pointing heavenwards to the top left corner. Notice how he's used white chalk to add highlights, contrasting with the dark shadows on the wrist.

3 | **Rembrandt, *Simeon and Jesus in the Temple*, c. mid-17th century:** The urgency of Rembrandt's pen strokes and the rough handling of the figures, particularly those on the right, suggest that the Dutchman was trying to organise the action within the picture frame, and so probably drew this as a study for a larger painting. The contrast between the foreground figures and those further away is stark, the sense of receding distance amplified by the empty space seen through the barely drawn architecture. For all its haste, this drawing has an undeniable warmth.

4 | **Canaletto, *Roman Ruins*, c. 1730:** This drawing depicts acutely observed crumbling ruins, a favourite theme of Italian artist Canaletto. The rich detail has been drawn in pen, while broad washes of diluted coloured ink underneath give a sense of solidity and depth. Human figures help to give the scene a sense of proportion and scale, dwarfed as they are by their surroundings. The main arch is drawn at an angle and is slightly off-centre so that the viewer's eye is led into and through the picture.

5 | **Hokusai, *Men and Women Dancing*, 1823:** Hokusai was from Japan, and is probably best known for his exquisitely simple prints, particularly *The Great Wave off Kanagawa*. This is a page from a sketchbook called 'Drawings in a Single Stroke of the Brush', and demonstrates how much expression and movement can be portrayed using the barest and most minimal of lines. Looking at the uncluttered purity of the figures, it's easy to make connections between an artist and the culture in which he or she was born and raised.

6 | **Van Gogh, *Fishing Boats on the Beach at Maries-de-la-Mer*, 1888:** Van Gogh was probably one of the first artists to see art as a vehicle for expression, and his drawings exemplify this as much as his more famous paintings. The lines describing these boats seem carved out of the same wood as the hulls themselves, their upper horizontal beams like the beaks of seagulls, the tide spilling out in a few watery pen strokes. Van Gogh clearly felt connected to his subject, and expresses it with a singular power.

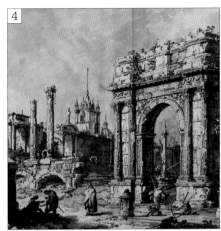

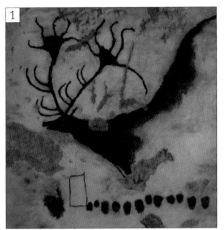

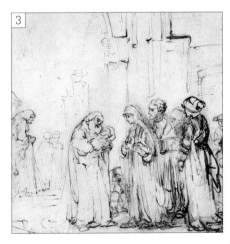

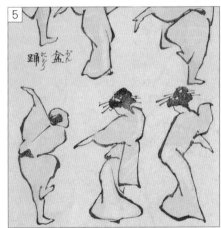

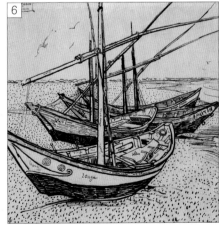

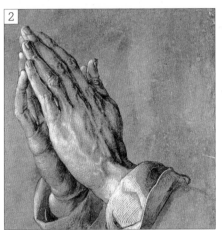

Looking at Drawing II

The idea of a book about drawing featuring imagery from places other than the usual gallery or museum may have some purists spurting cappuccino over themselves. It pays to keep your eyes open at all times, however, especially when seeking inspiration. Everyday pictures can have a power, grace and sophistication traditionally found only in the most revered fine-art pieces. Such imagery is cheap and easily accessible: start collecting favourite examples in a scrapbook and build up your own personal library.

1 **Map of the Planets:** This old celestial map provides an insight into how the world was once understood. It seems a million miles away from the spectacular imagery provided by NASA satellites nowadays, and is almost charmingly naïve. However, its design is fascinating to the point of abstraction, like a doodle gone awry, and the map is packed with a richly detailed flatness. Five hundred years from now, what are the chances that today's NASA imagery will seem as alien and misguided to people as this map appears to us?

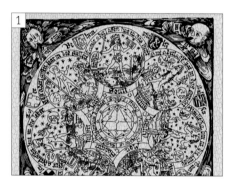

2 **Old Street Map of New York City:** A sense of nostalgia often comes through in old maps, particularly when the areas depicted have changed irrevocably. It speaks of another time, yet, because of its clarity and precision, it seems so full of authority as to be almost timeless. The cool blue water works with the grey urban sprawl, the gridded streets and straight lines contrasting with the sensual curves of the rivers, the clusters of text and line playing against the wider spaces that are free from development. Maps can indeed be seductive.

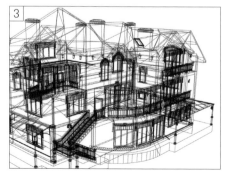

3 **Architectural Blueprint:** Obviously this has been made on a computer, but look carefully at the line width. The thicker lines are the most noticeable, the ones describing the front of the building. As it recedes, the lines get thinner – a handy trick to use when creating perspective. This is a complex drawing that reveals a huge amount of information about the structure, depicted with an utterly objective clarity and crispness.

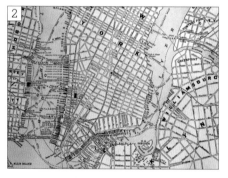

4 **Peace Sign:** A drawing of a symbol recognised the world over. That this one has been drawn in chalk (essentially compressed dust) only adds to its simplicity. We're used to chalk in the classroom, so it seems entirely appropriate that this person's desire for peace should be expressed with a kind of child-like innocence. Think about the materials you use in your drawings and how they can add weight to any message you may want to convey.

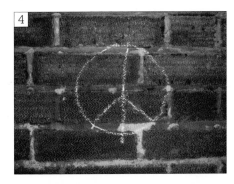

5 **'Let Sam Do It', Political Cartoon by Winsor McCay:** Cartooning has a long and illustrious history. Many well-known artists reached out to a huge audience using single-frame or strip cartoons. The graphic lines of artists as varied as McCay, James Gillray, Saul Steinberg, Charles Schulz and Gary Larson have entertained and outraged readers for centuries. Do you have any favourites? Do some research, look again at cartoonists' work, and think about why you like it.

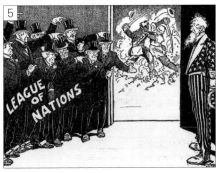

6 **U.S. Political Symbols:** These two symbols grew out of political cartoons from the 19th century. Since then, both the Democratic and Republican parties have represented themselves as the donkey and the elephant, respectively. Notice their simplicity and shape, and how the red, white and blue have been incorporated into the final design. Logos like these, and the peace sign above, are prime examples of how a drawing, when stripped to its bare essentials of form, can still carry a wealth of information and power.

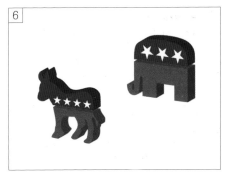

7 **Beanpod Botanical Illustration:** The subtle mark-making found in old prints such as this can easily inspire your own drawings. This beanpod has been rendered using just a series of dots (also known as stippling), giving the form weight and substance. This illustration owes much to the development of microscopes, and would have been drawn to show off the new technology as much as the natural form it depicted. Many artists have used such devices to create their own accurate drawings, often giving the work a cool, subjective feel.

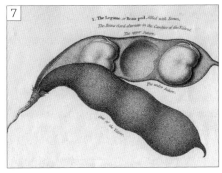

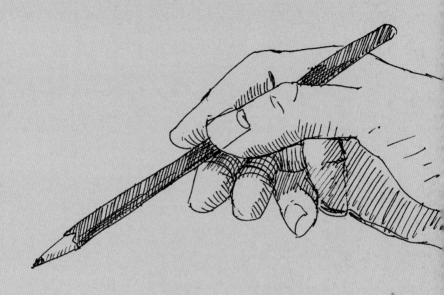

Before You Start

As with many things, preparation is key. This section will introduce you to the materials available to you as you start your drawing voyage. Visit your local art supplier and spend some time looking at what's on offer. Try things out before you buy them, and ask for assistance if necessary. It's a good idea to only go for the essentials at this early stage. As time goes on and you start to improve, the items kept in the shop's dustier corners should arouse your curiosity.

Pencils

Pencils are the tools most often associated with drawing, maybe because so many of us used them at school. They are versatile, sensual, fluid and mistakes are easy to correct with a rubber. They are, however, unforgiving in that even the slightest pressure will leave a mark; sensitivity is certainly required when using one.

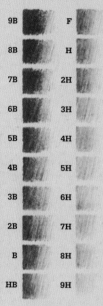

Comparable implements used by ancient civilisations tended to be thin metal sticks that would scratch the writing surface. It was, however, the discovery of a huge source of graphite in the early 1500s in Seathwaite, England, that led to today's pencil (at first it was used by the locals to mark their sheep). Graphite, a form of carbon, is soft and dark. After being ground to a powder and added to clay and water, it is then formed into long, thin spaghetti-like strings that are fired in a kiln. Once dipped in wax or oil, these rods are inserted between long planks of grooved juniper or incense cedar wood, glued together and then finally cut into pencils. For all our modern technology, the pencil-making process is remarkably similar to that used hundreds of years ago.

Pencil Grades

The amount of clay added determines the pencil's final hardness – more clay makes for a harder lead. Most pencils around the world are graded according to a European system of classification. Using the letters H ('hardness') and B ('blackness'), the hardest pencil available is a 9H, the softest a 9B, the most common an HB, and the one in between an F ('fine point'). Pencils can be used to make any number of marks on paper, and you should buy at least three of varying softness to play around with and find out what suits you and your subjects best. Harder pencils are generally favoured by designers and engineers, as they give greater control; artists may prefer the softer, more expressive tones of the B pencils. Nothing is fixed in stone, though, and there are no laws forbidding you from using two or more pencil grades in one drawing.

TRY THIS . . .

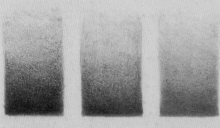

6B tone   2B tone   1H tone

Tone: Create areas of tone to familiarise yourself with how each pencil behaves. As you move to the right of the paper, increase the pressure. Get your eyes up close to the surface so you can see what's going on and be aware of the relationship between your hand and eye, the pencil and the paper. Notice how, in the example, the 6B gives a very rich tone, while the H is decidedly cold.

6B marks

   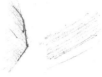

2B marks

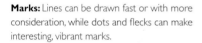

1H marks

Marks: Lines can be drawn fast or with more consideration, while dots and flecks can make interesting, vibrant marks.

Smudges: Once you've got the pencil down, smudging it can create new areas of softer value, as seen in the sketch of a sphere on the right. Use a cotton bud or tissue rolled to a point. You can also use your fingers, though take extra care in more delicate areas – fingers are notoriously difficult to control.

Smudges

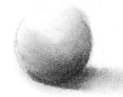

Rubber: Another way of reworking pencil is to use a rubber. Areas can be softened and texture added. Experiment with the hard edge of a plastic rubber (below left) or a soft, kneadable putty rubber (below right).

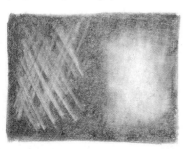

Sharpening

Standard metal sharpeners are great for a regular, clean line. Using a sharp craft knife, however, will enable you to determine exactly what sort of point or wedge shape you require – at least, once you've mastered the technique.

Charcoal and Pastels

Both charcoal and pastels have a similar tactile quality. They are sensitive media that respond to the tiniest amount of pressure, and often leave you, if not your drawing, covered in their remnants. Care therefore needs to be taken when using them, but their soft sensuality can add a wealth of feeling to your work.

Charcoal

Charcoal is a sensitive, expressive medium readily found in most art supply shops. Like graphite, it is derived from carbon, though its structure is very different. This makes it even more responsive and less forgiving, and you'll probably find your fingers play as much a part in creating a charcoal drawing as the stick itself.

One of the most primal of materials, charcoal is essentially burnt wood. Cave paintings dating back to 30000 B.C.E. were made using the ends of charred sticks taken directly from the fire. Charcoal later became an essential element in the smelting of bronze and iron, and is now used in heating, horticulture and medicine, as well as art.

Artists from the Renaissance onwards have exploited charcoal's dust-like, 'barely there' qualities when making preparatory drawings.

Later developments to 'fix' the material to the paper meant it could be used to make more finished, detailed drawings in their own right. Spray-on fixative is now standard for sealing the image and ensuring an afterlife.

There are two main varieties: vine (also known as 'willow') charcoal, which comes in fragile sticks of varying thicknesses; and compressed charcoal, whereby the charcoal powder is mixed with a gum binder, resulting in a darker, harder, sturdier stick or pencil. At first, charcoal may seem unwieldy and messy; it certainly favours a bold, direct way of working on larger pieces of paper. Practice will make it easier to manipulate and, once grasped, its soft, sensitive properties will come into their own. Using charcoal is also a good way of investigating the breadth of tonal values.

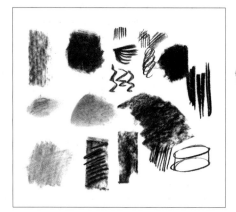

Charcoal

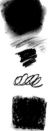

Compressed charcoal

TRY THIS . . .

Given its fragility, a charcoal stick should be held gently and loosely. Lay an area of charcoal down on paper, focusing on how it can be worked, layered and shifted. Then experiment with ways of removing it – a rubber, your fingers, an old rag or even day-old bread moulded to a tip can be used to lift the dust and work your way back into what you've drawn.

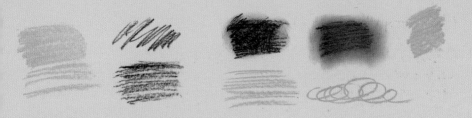

Chalk Pastels

Belonging to a similarly smudgy family as charcoal, chalk (or 'soft') pastels can bring a whole range of colour to your drawing. They are available in full-strength pigments as well as shades and tints, and come either in blocks or pencils. Different techniques have different effects: use the side of a pastel block to create larger areas of colour and the end for sharper detail; layering two or more colours will add depth to your drawing, as will increasing the pressure as you draw. Gently rubbing a tissue or piece of cloth or cotton pad into the pastel will give you a much softer tone. If money's tight, try the same techniques with a box of regular blackboard chalks (white chalk can be used to lift and lighten charcoal and other similarly dark materials).

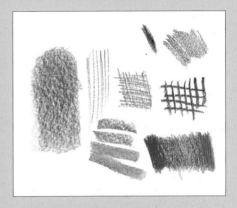

Oil Pastels

Whereas chalk pastels consist of pigment bound with gum, oil pastels are bound with oil and wax. This gives them a buttery, malleable consistency, making them more resilient and their colours more intense. They are harder to blend than their chalk counterparts – choose instead to layer them. Be aware that heat can make them sticky, both on the paper and on your fingers – cool your hands in cold water before you use them if necessary.

Fixative

Both charcoal and chalk pastels generate a lot of dust when used, so you need to be careful to avoid breathing too much in. Work in a well-ventilated area, if possible. Similarly, once the drawing is completed it will be susceptible to even the slightest knock or smudge. A light layer of fixative will seal the material to the paper – spray evenly over the paper, going from top to bottom and, again, go easy on the fume intake. Finished pencil drawings will also benefit from being sealed in this way.

Pen and Ink

Ink favours the brave. Once it hits the paper, that's it – there's no way back. No rubber will remove what you've done. Working in ink therefore forces you to look a lot more closely at your subject, build on the relationship you have with it, and commit yourself fully to the drawing at hand. While this may sound daunting, the upside is a more confident, decisive way of working – and of course, there's always room for one or two mistakes.

Inks

There are many different kinds of ink and, for such an apparently simple material, an impressive variety of components. Varying quantities of pigments, dyes, resins, solvents, lubricants and fluorescers (among others) all help to control the flow of ink, its consistency and how fast it dries. Throughout history, a similarly wide range of strange ingredients have been used. Burnt bones, tar, berries, animal musk, soot, graphite, iron salts, gallnuts and hawthorn bark have all been used at various times by different cultures from as early as the 12th century B.C.E. to make marks on stone, parchment or paper.

India ink is, however, the standard used by most artists today. It is commonly used in a diluted form and dries with a slight sheen. A non-waterproof version can be further diluted with more water and applied with a brush to give you a variety of finishes and tones. Use a dip pen with a steel nib (available in different widths) to play around with the various possibilities for mark-making.

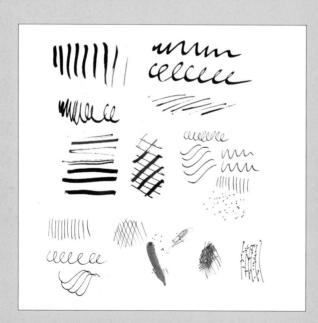

As you see from these scribbles, various nib widths will give you a whole range of marks.

TRY THIS . . .

Avoid the trap of thinking you need to buy a huge array of pens, particularly if you're just starting out. Buy two or three that you like, preferably of varying thickness, and play around with how they feel. Even an apparently mindless doodle will reveal the capabilities of each pen. This knowledge will help you when it comes to making more detailed drawings later.

Pens

Ink carriers have evolved through a number of different permutations and manifestations over the years. Pens fashioned from a single reed straw and bamboo lengths were common in ancient Egypt, and quills made from the feathers of various birds were used to write some of the Dead Sea Scrolls circa 100 B.C.E. The advent of metal nibs in the early 19th century enabled a smoother flow of ink to the paper and less transmission of ink to the fingers. As literacy and social mobility increased in the 20th century, so did the development of cheaper, portable pens, such as the ballpoint, the rollerball and the marker.

There is still a huge variety of pens available. Fine-line (or technical) pens are available in a series of widths and give a consistent, clean line and a 'graphic' finish. Felt-tip pens can enliven a drawing with different colours and marks (they come with thin, thick or brush lines). Even a humble ballpoint or rollerball can be especially useful for quick sketches and scribbles in your sketch pad.

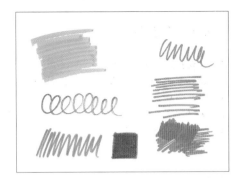

Felt-tip pen

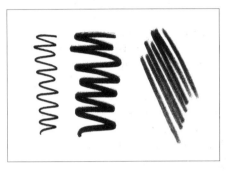

Marker pen

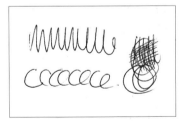

Rollerball pen

Mistakes

Don't be intimidated by the fact that you can't rub out a pen drawing. As already mentioned, it can really force you to look hard at what you're drawing. If you make a mistake, it's not the end of the world — mistakes are all part of learning. If your final picture contains them (and what picture doesn't?), use and embrace them — they are part of you and the art you make.

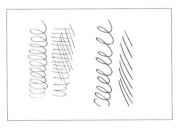

Fibre-tip pen

Crayon

The word *crayon* may very well conjure up images of waxy cylindrical sticks used to scrawl mad lines on a big piece of paper in the classroom. The range of crayons is much wider than you may remember; indeed, some crayons could now even be called sophisticated. Strictly speaking, the term *crayon* describes any drawing material in stick form. As charcoal and pastels have already been discussed, let's limit ourselves to a few other examples.

Wax Crayons

Wax crayons are perfect for kids – they are immediate, hassle-free and non-toxic. Made from mixing paraffin and chemical pigments, wax crayons have been around since the late 19th century, though the Egyptians were the first to use ink and beeswax together in creating art. They are not such a popular medium among artists, possibly because of their unforgiving nature and their limited expressive qualities, certainly compared to, say, something like a chalk pastel. The wax crayon could therefore be a really useful tool for the beginner intimidated by the sheer breadth of what's available at the 'upper end' of drawing materials. Use it to loosen up tight fingers and just enjoy the simple process of looking and drawing what you see.

Pencil Crayons

Otherwise known as coloured pencils, pencil crayons were first produced in the early years of the 20th century, initially as markers, then soon after for artistic use in both America and Europe. They are made in much the same way as regular pencils, except that their leads avoid

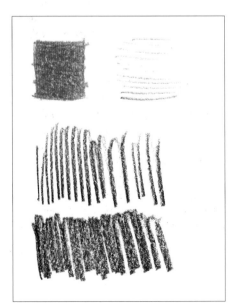

Wax crayon

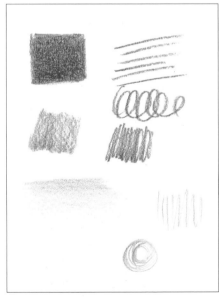

Pencil crayon

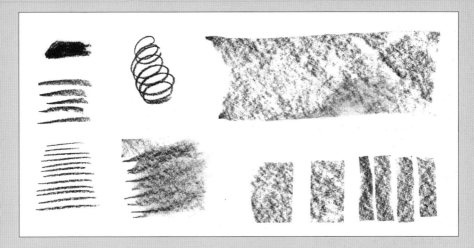

Conté crayon

the kiln, as the firing would damage the pigments. It is the proportion of these fairly expensive pigments within each pencil that determines its quality. Usually sold in sets of anything up to 120 pencils, some of the higher-range pencil crayons are also available individually, making them easily replaceable. They are expressive and easy to use and transport, though mistakes, especially those in heavy layers of colour, are difficult to erase. You will also be limited in how many layers of crayon you can put down before the surface of the paper becomes shiny. Areas of water-soluble pencil crayon can be reworked with a brush, allowing for a greater variety of finishes.

Conté Crayons

Conté crayons were developed in France after the Napoleonic Wars of 1795 prevented the import of graphite from England. Nicolas-Jacques Conté created a new type of crayon that would carry his name: sticks containing small amounts of graphite kiln-fired with clay. The traditional (and still most popular) Conté colours are earthy: sanguine (terracotta red), sepia (warm brown), bistre (cool brown) and black and white, though a greater range of colours has become available over the past few years. Like a cross between a pastel and a pencil, Conté crayons are soft to use while allowing for a high range of detail, and along with different colours, there are varying degrees of hardness. They are usually used with thick paper, as the pigment connects well with the rough grain. Coloured paper can also add something extra to the final work. Contés can be messy, so keep the drawing as dust-free and clean as possible.

Paper and Other Surfaces

It certainly helps to think about what you're drawing on, as well as what you're drawing with, particularly once you hit your stride and can draw with a degree of confidence and commitment. Obviously you have the sketch pad that comes with this book to help start your expedition into drawing, but further into the journey you'll want to try new things.

Paper

Paper is produced by compressing wood pulp fibres. Size, weight, texture and colour are the four major considerations when choosing paper. Most art suppliers will be well stocked with a full range – something for all levels and budgets. These days a ream (500 sheets) can cost little more than a cup of coffee; a far cry from mid-15th-century Europe, when one high-quality sheet would set you back the equivalent of an average weekly wage. Paper sizing follows a logic born out of necessity

– namely, how to get as much paper as possible out of a particular size sheet. Somewhat confusingly, the United States, Canada and Mexico follow one system, while countries in the rest of the world follow the ISO, or International Organisation for Standardisation (with variants in certain countries). Shown below are two common sizing charts: the ANSI (American National Standards Institute) and the ISO A.

Paper weight follows two similarly separate systems. In the United States, it is given as the

The ANSI and ISO A (right) standard paper sizes.

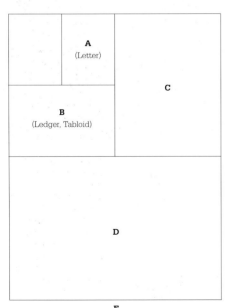

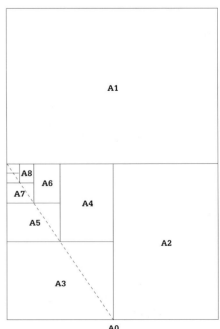

weight of a ream of basic sizes; elsewhere it is expressed as grammes per square metre (gsm). Thicker, more substantial paper will take more punishment, so use it for more detailed work or for drawing with tools such as coloured pencils and pastels. Something thinner, like newsprint, is useful for jotting down quick sketches and ideas, and tracing paper always helps if you want to try out new ideas or transfer images.

Paper also comes in a variety of finishes, often determined by the way the sheets are heat-treated at the mill. Certain coatings can also be used. As a guide, choose a rougher finish if working with softer materials like pastels, as the grain traps the pigment better. Slightly smoother paper works best for something like charcoal, while an all-purpose, smooth cartridge paper is great for any pencil and ink work. Most shops will have sample sheets for you to feel and scribble on before you buy and, of course, there are no rules you have to follow – only your personal preferences are important when choosing paper.

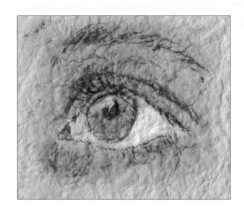

Other Surfaces

While paper is certainly the best material to draw on, there are always alternatives. Cardboard, napkins, toilet tissue, canvas and scratchboards provide new challenges and rewards. You may also want to start experimenting with layers of paper or collage.

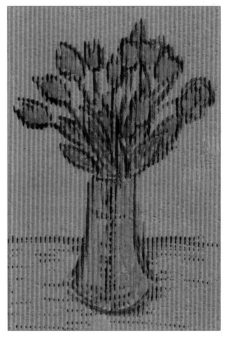

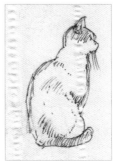

Not having a smooth, pure surface needn't prevent you from drawing; other textures can add a whole new level to your work. Examples shown here, from the top, include handmade paper, corrugated cardboard and toilet tissue.

Grip and Pressure

Art is very much about the relationship between the work and its creator. There is only you and your drawing, until you decide to release it from your care and let it make its own way into the world. As much as this book can show you ways to do things, there is no right or wrong way. This applies across the board, but is especially important when it comes to how you hold your drawing medium of choice.

Certainly, when we first start writing and drawing, there can be some concern over how we hold our pencils. A poor grip can lead to uncontrolled, nervous, or untidy marks; taken into adulthood, it can cause unnecessary tension in the joints of the hand. When I was growing up, a teacher or parent would often comment on the way I held my pencil, as it looked a little different. Indeed, years down the line, my own personal grip is still something of a variation on a theme. So while it's important to consider your method, I'd also suggest that forcing yourself into changing something for the sake of doing it 'properly' could do more harm than good. Be aware of the different ways you can hold and control (or otherwise) your medium; play around with it, but note that an artificial grip will probably lead to marks that feel foreign, cramped and stressed.

The most standard grip is the *tripod*. The pencil is held with equal pressure from the thumb, the side of the middle finger, and the tip of the index finger. The little and ring fingers support the middle finger. The pencil can be readily controlled in this way, which is perfect for drawing fine detail.

Holding the pencil further up the shaft will free your hand and allow for more open marks. The smallest of finger movements will make the pencil swing wider and mark lighter, so it is an economical grip for sketching and can be useful for roughing out basic elements of a composition, for example.

The overhand grip works well if there is some distance between you and your drawing surface (if you're standing at an easel, for example). The pencil rests against all fingers and is held by the thumb and index finger. This position can free up your hand and arm

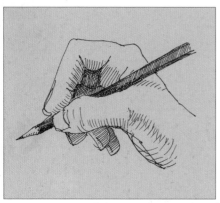

Tripod grip

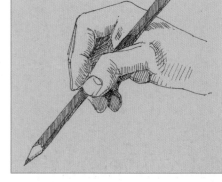

Higher grip

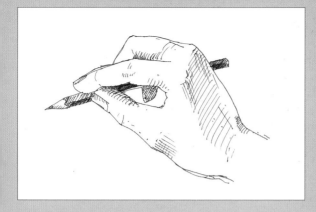

Overhand

TRY THIS . . .

Take a pencil and, holding it in the various ways shown here, experiment with mark-making. Move your wrist, your elbow, and your shoulder and sit or stand away from the paper at various distances. How does it feel? Are the marks made worth pursuing?

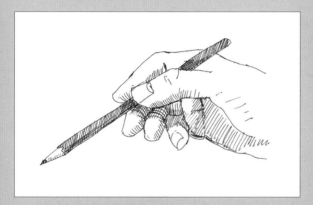

Underhand

considerably, and allows you to shade comfortably with the side of the pencil.

When you're working with charcoal, you could try the underhand grip. It's essentially a turned tripod grip in which the edge of the hand is in contact with the paper. The thumb holds the stick, or whatever you're using, against the tops of the index and middle fingers, and makes for a very loose and relaxed grip.

If you're working with pastels, don't forget that you can use the side of the stick as well as the top. Slide it along the paper to leave broad bands of colour, then rub over it with a cotton pad, tissue or your fingers if you're after a smoother finish.

Pressure

Not all implements respond well to increasing the pressure on the paper. Press too hard with a fibre-tip pen, for example, and you run the risk of ruining the nib. Softer media will let you treat them considerably rougher. Pressing harder with a pastel ups the level of pigment (and dust) deposited, and while a pencil demands some sensitivity, you can certainly achieve a wide variety of tones and finishes by altering how hard you press. As ever, when using a new material, give yourself a few minutes to hold it and test it on a scrap piece of paper to get to know it.

Subject Selection

Earlystage artists will want to keep progressing and learning with each new drawing, and should keep things simple to start with. Choosing something to draw should, in theory, be pretty easy – there is loads of stuff in the world, after all. Ask yourself a few questions before you start to help focus you on the job at hand and what you want to achieve: What does the subject look like? What materials will be most appropriate? How much time have you got? Always look at your subject for a few minutes before committing anything to paper.

Looking at nature has long been an essential part of an artist's development. The majority of man-made items have flat surfaces, straight edges, and a certain symmetry (a fork is a fork is a fork), while no two trees, for example, are ever the same. More organic subjects have a rich diversity of form, weight, and texture to explore and convey. Nature is also a more forgiving subject – you can edit, draw and redraw, leave bits out, put bits in; your drawing will still portray the essence of the subject.

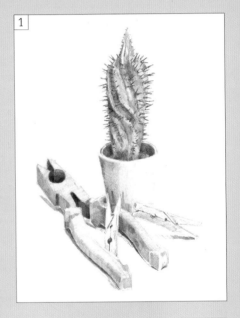

Genres

Much traditional artistic practice is classified into various genres: still life, portraiture, landscape, and the figure – each with its own merits, challenges, and pitfalls.

1 Still life

Useful for indoor study, and leaves you plenty of time to work. You call the shots in terms of layout, lighting, and so on, and it can be returned to time and time again (providing the setup remains undisturbed). Good for understanding how shapes and forms relate to each other, and how light works.

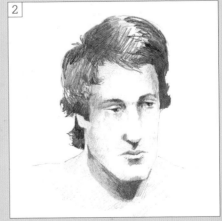

2 Portrait

If the eyes are the window to the soul, then maybe the face is the whole house. Because we all have one, drawing a face, either your own or someone else's, can be particularly intimidating. Slight errors make huge differences. That said, portrait drawing improves the way we look at things and raises awareness of the interrelation of different forms.

3 Landscape

Urban, rural or somewhere in between – landscape drawings take us out of ourselves and force us to look at the world around us. Practical considerations such as the weather, the light, the portability of your materials, where to sit, and so on, make preparation key. It's a robust way of working that helps us with perspective and composition especially.

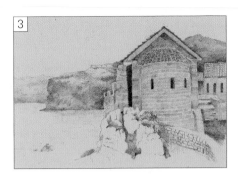

4 The Figure

As with the face, our own lived-in body can prevent us from looking at someone else's with fresh eyes. There are considerable rewards in producing a successful figure drawing, though – you learn to examine and harmonise the different parts of the body while understanding the form in front of you, and by extension your own. Look for life drawing classes in your village, town or city.

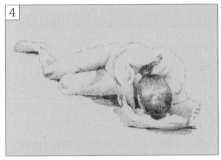

5 Photographs

Some artists and teachers are sniffy about drawing from photographs. It certainly feels different to make a 2D image from another 2D image, and can lead to a 'flatter' image that lacks the dynamics of three dimensions. However, you may very well find it easier, more practical or even desirable to produce a drawing that is based on a photograph. It's your call, but do give drawing from the real, the fleshy, and the earthly a go – if only to find out you don't like it.

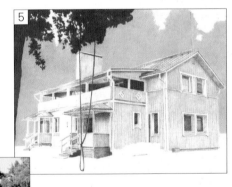

TRY THIS . . .

Put this book down and grab a piece of paper and something to draw with. Look at the book for a minute or two, then start to draw its outline. Think about the book as you continue to draw – the cover, the pages, how it looks, and how it feels. Don't spend too much time on it – this exercise is intended to show you that inspiration can come from anywhere.

Lighting

All of the different aspects involved in drawing will be discussed in the following chapters, but it's worth taking a moment here to talk briefly about lighting. Light plays an essential part in how we recognise and understand objects, and as your observational skills develop, so will your awareness of the role light plays. Different light sources can have a major impact on the process of drawing, as well as how the final work will look, so it's a good idea to give it some thought before you start.

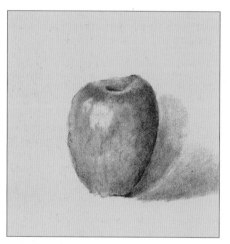

Natural light

Natural Light

Natural light is a soft, organic light, and will invest your drawing with these qualities should you decide to work with it. At best, a single source of light (maybe from a window) should illuminate both your subject and your drawing. Don't forget that as the day progresses, the light source will shift position, and its intensity will diminish. Either work fast or come back to your subject around the same time each day until the drawing is finished.

Artificial Light

Drawing using solely artificial light will afford you much greater control over the final work. Use an everyday desk lamp (one that allows a variety of positions, if possible) to create your own setting and establish the drawing's atmosphere. Make sure there is enough light for you to see what you're doing as well. Artificial light is direct and consistent, and it allows you to return to the drawing whenever you wish. It is also stronger and harsher than natural light, so it creates deeper shadows and brighter highlights. Light can also come from different directions:

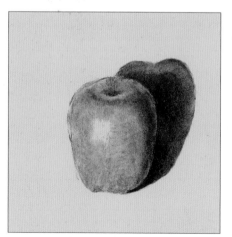

Artificial light

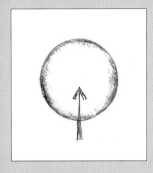

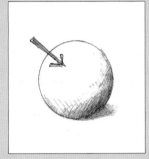

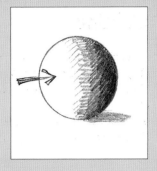

Front Light

Front light provides an effect similar to a harsh flash on a photograph. Seeing the tonal detail may be harder as a result, although some shadows will fall at the subject's edges. Front light is great if you only want to concentrate on outline.

Form Light

Many traditional painters like Rembrandt and Vermeer used form light, capturing both light and shade on the same subject. The light comes in over the artist's shoulder, and neither swamps nor bisects the subject. Form light is particularly flattering to the face.

Side Light

Side light comes in straight onto the side of the subject, resulting in a half-and-half appearance that can create some atmospheric effects. It can strengthen the contrast between light and dark as well as show form.

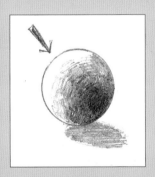

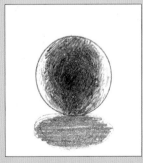

Rim Light

Similar to form light, here the subject is lit from above and behind. This casts a large part of it in shadow as you see it, with a sliver of light cast on the upper corner.

Back Light

Backlit subjects are heavily shadowed, so tonal ranges should be carefully observed. What light is visible can provide an exciting contrast. Remember that figures that are backlit are usually the villains of the piece.

TRY THIS . . .

Take this book, place it by a window, and observe where its shadow falls in relation to the light outside. Then find a darker room and light the book with a desk lamp or flashlight. Observe again the changes in the shadows – their intensity and their position. Bear in mind that the further away the light source, the more the light will be suffused.

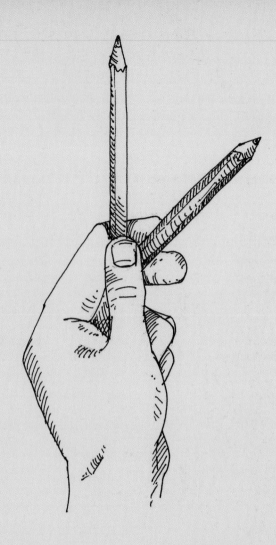

Starting

You've chosen your subject and your materials. You've found a comfortable place to sit, and the lighting is just right. What comes next – making the first mark – can be something of a stumbling block, so this section is designed to ease you into the drawing process. If each picture is a building, think of these pages as the foundation.

Layout

Much more will be discussed about this topic in the Composition section starting on page 64, but it is useful to talk a bit about basic layout ideas here as you start to consider exactly where and how your drawing will fit onto the blank rectangle in front of you.

Planning and Playing

Take a good look at your subject. You are the artist, creator, director – you choose what is to go where and how it will all fit together. It's a drawing, not a photograph, so you are free to discard anything you think may disturb your enjoyment as you make the drawing, or the viewer's as they look at it. You are similarly free to draw your subject from any number of angles. What happens when you place your still life arrangement at your feet? Or when you move to the side of the sitter so that their face is revealed in profile? If you shift your chair slightly, are any interesting bits in the landscape unexpectedly revealed? Be playful and take an active role in determining exactly how this drawing will turn out. Using a viewfinder can help you enormously in this respect (see page 40 for more details).

Format

Once you've decided on your main focus, decide on the format of your piece of paper. It is a rectangle with two options: portrait (lengthwise) or landscape (widthwise). You may also want to follow Andy Warhol, who said, 'I like [...] a square because you don't have to decide whether it should be longer-longer or shorter-shorter or longer-shorter: it's just a square'.

Landscape

Portrait

Square

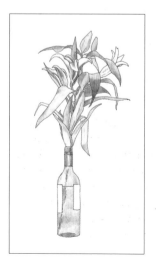

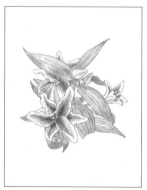

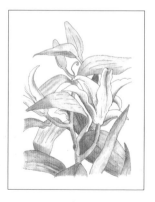

A bunch of flowers in a bottle, seen from three different viewpoints: a straightforward profile shot (left); a view of the arrangement from above (centre); and a close-up detail (right).

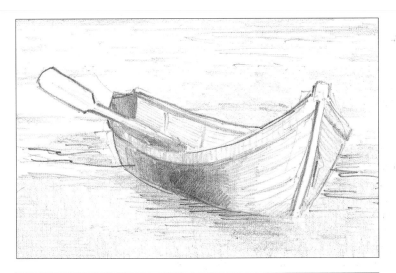

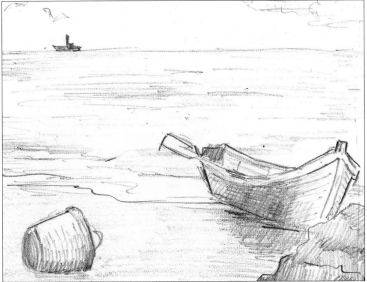

The Eye

There are certain rules concerning how the eye works that you can exploit to create a more aesthetically pleasing drawing. The eye is immediately drawn to any focal point or centre of interest, be it a particularly large tree, a very shiny fork or a dazzlingly drawn pair of eyes. Advertisers obviously exploit this by using larger text for their most important slogans and messages. Try to avoid slapping your focal point in the middle of your drawing, however – give it room to breathe and try to include some visual stepping stones (secondary focal points) to lead the viewer into and around the picture. Consider the example above – the addition of the rock, fishing basket, and distant ship creates more interest than the boat on its own.

Viewfinders and Grids

There are ways and means of getting your drawn subject to resemble the real thing – it's not just a case of being incredibly gifted. Simple rules and methods, like the viewfinder and the grid, can ease the burden of creating an accurate drawing, freeing you to explore other areas of investigation once the bare bones have been laid down.

The Viewfinder

Before starting, you can mimic the edges of your piece of paper by creating a portable frame. Holding this frame up to your subject will then help you focus on what to draw and what to leave out. A bit of judicious editing never did anyone any harm, and it can make life a lot easier for you.

Cut out two L-shaped pieces of cardpaper. Black is probably the best colour, as it will throw everything into sharp relief, but it's not essential. Hold the pieces up in front of you to create a rectangular aperture that echoes the shape of your paper (landscape, portrait or square). You can then move them around your chosen subject – be it a still life, landscape or figure – and find what, for you, provides the most interest. Look for the focal points we discussed on the previous page and how they fit in with the rest of the frame.

Once you've chosen your area, mark out on the paper where the corners of your subject are. Looking back at your subject, you should see the viewfinder's edges in your mind's eye, helping you root the image on the paper.

The Grid

You can then make life even easier by drawing a faint grid onto the paper. Think of how much easier maps are to read if they are divided into more manageable squares or rectangles. This is the same procedure. Once you've settled on your subject, divide the paper in half vertically, then horizontally. The resulting quarters effectively break down the complexity of the subject into four separate elements that are easier to focus on. Refer back to the viewfinder to work out, for example, the central elements of your drawing, and you will find plotting the design of your image a lot easier.

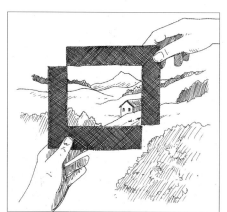

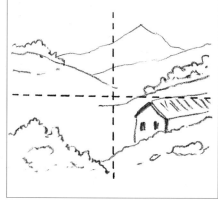

How to Make a Combined Viewfinder/Grid

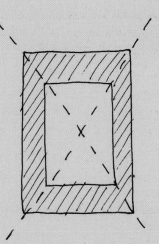

1 Trace the outline of your piece of paper onto the back of an old cereal box or similar object, and cut it out. With a ruler, draw diagonal lines to the opposite corners. In the centre, draw a rectangle that uses the diagonal lines as the base for its corners (this ensures that the viewfinder will match the proportions of the paper). Then cut out the rectangle.

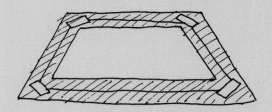

2 Next, cut a sheet of clear plastic to a size slightly larger than the aperture. Stick it onto the viewfinder with tape and draw a grid on it with a marker pen. Draw a corresponding grid with the same number of squares onto the paper.

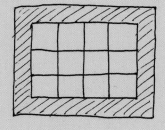

3 Lift your viewfinder/grid up to your subject, then look back at your paper: it should be apparent how you can map the edges and main features of your subject onto the paper with ease and a fair degree of accuracy.

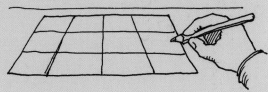

Measuring and Proportion

It's usually important for a two-dimensional drawing to accurately convey the way things are in the three-dimensional world. Capturing things on paper depends on a successful depiction of their proportions; namely, the relationship between parts of the same object, and the distance relationship between one object and another.

Taking Measurements

If you imagine an artist drawing something, you may very well picture him or her sticking an arm out at various intervals with a pencil in hand. What they are doing is not a fancy ritual, but rather 'sighting', a very useful trick to get the right measurements and proportions. It requires no technical equipment or thinking, and is a foolproof method for ensuring that things on paper appear as they are in reality.

In following this method, you should always keep your head still and both the subject matter and the drawing in clear view. Always hold your hand out at arm's length (in other words, don't sit too close to your subject) and keep your elbow straight at all times. If you bend your elbow, you risk getting a different measurement each time.

Sighting can be an essential tool for all artists. With practice, you will probably find that your ability to perceive distance and form will improve greatly and your reliance on sighting will diminish. Even when you're not using it much, it's still very satisfying to use this method, just to prove that you're on the right track.

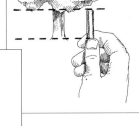

A section of your chosen medium, measured carefully against a small part of your subject, can be used to plot out the rest of your drawing.

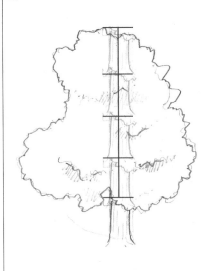

1 **A tree**

We want to draw a tree with a short trunk and a large, leafy canopy. Look closely at the trunk, then draw it. This is now your basic unit for measuring the height of the whole tree. Hold your pencil out at arm's length, close one eye and align the pencil end with the top of the visible trunk. Now slide your thumb up or down the pencil shaft so it aligns with the bottom of the trunk. Then, keeping your thumb in place, measure how many 'trunks' fit into the canopy, one on top of the other. This can then be applied to your drawing, giving you a pretty accurate depiction of the trunk in relation to the whole tree. Here, the canopy is four trunks high.

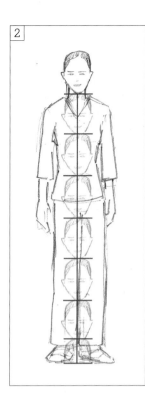

2 The figure

This time the head of our model will be our basic unit to measure the height of the whole figure. Just a rough outline will do – detail can be added later. As a rule, the standing human body is seven-and-a-half heads tall (though shapes vary, and different poses will affect the height). With arm out and one eye closed, line up your head measurement with your thumb and pencil, move the pencil top down to the chin and notice where the next 'head' falls. On your drawing, mark this off and repeat the process until the full figure is mapped out on the paper. You can also turn the pencil horizontally to measure how many 'heads' fill the width of the model.

TRY THIS . . .

Take this book and stand it on its end. Sit back from it with a pencil and piece of paper and use the sighting method to plot how the book fills the space around it.

3 A group of objects

Use sighting to understand the relationship between various objects. Use a roughly drawn small item as your unit to measure the height and width of other items, as well as the gaps between them. In this example, three-and-a-half 'kiwi fruits' occupy the distance between the edge of the picture frame and the flowerpot.

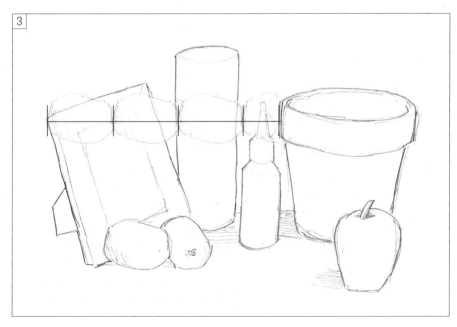

Angles

Drawing angles correctly can make a big difference to the readability of your final image. Be it the back of a chair or the bend of a leg, getting it wrong can scupper what might otherwise be a decent picture. Making an effort, especially early on as you plot the basic layout, can save you a lot of hassle and correction later on and give your drawing a convincing dynamism.

Just as the pencil in your hand can be used to measure distance and proportion (see the previous spread), so it can be teamed up with another to form a kind of floating protractor. Hold two pencils out in front of you as shown, keeping your elbow straight. Ensure that the first one is held vertically (measure it against the frame of a door or window to be sure), then move the second pencil so it aligns with the angle you want to draw. Carefully lower your pencil angle to your drawing and draw the required line.

Alternatively, and similarly to the viewfinder on page 40, you could make your own movable protractor. Cut two lengths of cardpaper as shown, sized so they fit comfortably in your hand. Place one on top of the other and drive a split pin through one of the ends. Holding your protractor at the base with your non-drawing hand at arm's length, turn the card arms so they match the angle required. Lower it to your picture and draw accordingly.

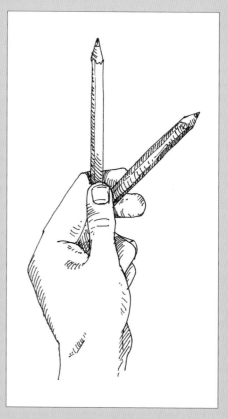

Carefully held pencils (or similar) can help you work out a tricky angle. Keep your hand and the pencils as steady as possible.

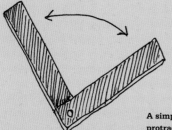

A simpler device is the homemade movable protractor. By getting the angles right, your drawings should look more convincing and life-like.

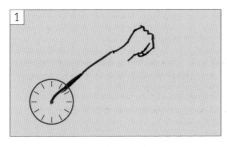

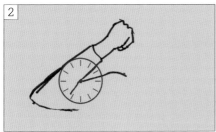

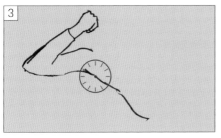

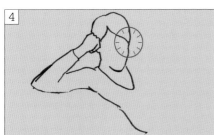

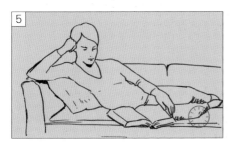

The Clock Face

Both of the previous methods are somewhat cumbersome and fiddly when you consider that we all have an easily accessible, ready-to-use set of angles in our own heads: those made by the hands of a clock. Having learned to tell time from an early age, the clock face is a familiar, easily recalled symbol for pretty much all of us. When faced with an angle that we may not have complete confidence in drawing, imagine a clock face superimposed over it. The direction of the line you need to draw is, essentially, the direction of the little hand.

Look at the example here. The drawing starts with the top line of the forearm sitting at an angle that is roughly that made by a clock's little hand when the time is 1:30. Having drawn the rest of the forearm, the line of the upper arm to the shoulder sits at about 2:30. The line leading down from the sitter's armpit lies at about 4:00, the left-hand side of the head is at 6:00 and finally, the line leading from the right knee up to the book sits at approximately 08:30.

TRY THIS . . .

Find a very simple, relatively flat object like a mobile phone or pencil and set it down in front of you. Draw just its outline. Now turn it a few degrees clockwise and draw it again. Repeat the exercise, turning and drawing, until the object has been turned a full 360 degrees. As you do this, refer back to the first drawing you made and notice the relation of its new angle to the original. Also think about how these angles relate to those made by the hands of the clock.

Copying and Tracing

Copying or tracing another drawing or photograph has had some bad press in certain circles. The practice goes against the idea of the Artist with a capital A, a maverick, a genius, a magician whose greatness would somehow be tainted by such an easy trick. This is despite the swell of evidence suggesting that many of the greats throughout history frequently used optical tricks and devices to help them draw, and for centuries copying from the Masters was a standard part of an artistic education.

Learning to draw is about training your eyes to see and your fingers to translate what you see onto paper. Copying and tracing can greatly improve your own artistic practice if you do it well, and with full awareness and concentration. Such methods will familiarise you with the practice of drawing without the pressure of getting it 'right' from the beginning. They'll also give you confidence in using various media, and recognising basic forms and how they interrelate.

The Grid

As discussed on page 40, a grid can really help root you to the job at hand by breaking your subject down into a series of more manageable chunks, particularly if you're working from a photograph or other drawing.

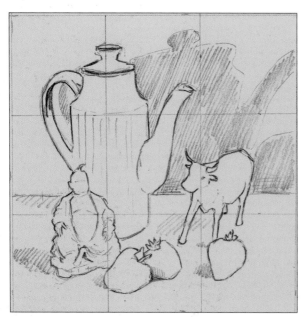

The grid can be particularly useful when your subject contains different shapes or features. It's a handy structure from which your subsequent drawing can hang.

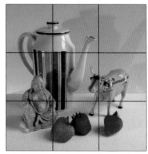

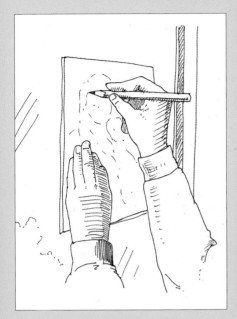

Tracing

Tracing is a very easy way to get the bare bones of your drawing onto the paper without worrying about it looking odd or unconvincing. Tracing paper can be easily used, and is readily available from art shops. If the final drawing is to be on thinner paper, place the paper over the image to be traced and put

both on top of a piece of glass with some kind of light source behind it. Lightboxes are available, but it is much cheaper to stick the original image onto a window, put the paper on top, then trace away.

Lessons from History?

British artist David Hockney caused something of a storm in 2001 with the publication of his book *Secret Knowledge*, and indeed, the storm still rages. In it, he and physicist Charles Falco posited the idea that some of the most notable artists from the Renaissance onwards used various optical tricks and devices to achieve the illusion of realism in their work, as opposed to the previously held idea that it was all due to talent and skill. They argue that aids such as the camera obscura and curved mirrors were used to project images of the sitters of van Eyck, Caravaggio and Ingres (among many others). These artists then traced the outlines onto their canvases. Their argument is robust and has ruffled many feathers, particularly among art historians who believe that the findings somehow tarnish the reputations of these artists. As you'll discover for yourself if you give it a go, it is one thing to trace an image, but another thing entirely to create something memorable from it.

TRY THIS . . .

Get a hold of a book of Old Master drawings, either from a bookshop or library. Failing that, many high-quality reproductions are available these days on the Internet – print one or two at home. Now either copy or trace what you see. The aim here is not simply to replicate the work, but to understand the artist's marks and how they came to be. Look closely, take your time and try to get into the head of the artist.

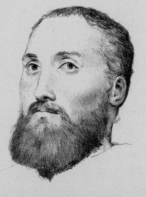

By copying old works, as I did here with a portrait from the School of Hans Holbein, you start to appreciate the skill and craft of past masters.

Approaches to Drawing

A successful drawing isn't just about capturing a life-like resemblance; it can equally express something about you and your relationship to your subject. The approaches to drawing detailed here offer a different model for how to draw, and introduce a new way of understanding the drawing process.

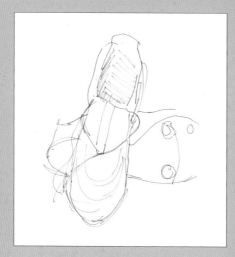

Gesture Drawing

Gesture drawing encourages you to think about your subject in terms other than appearance. It is an approach related to certain Eastern belief systems in which everything – animal, vegetable, mineral – has an essence, an inner energy that resonates throughout the universe. Gesture drawing helps you find that essence and commit it to paper.

No fancy kit is needed to make a gesture drawing. Any medium will do – just a standard piece of paper and your eyes, and you're ready to go. And anything can be your subject. The focus here is on looking closely and acutely, almost to the point where your pencil or pen is following the direction of your eyes as they scan your subject. In a sense you're aiming to bypass your brain – you are like an empty vessel channelling the subject onto the paper. Avoid looking at the paper too much – short glances are all you need, as the primary focus should be your subject.

Soccer boots, a corn cob, yourself – the subject of gesture drawing is not as important as the way it is made. Keep your drawing medium fluid and free.

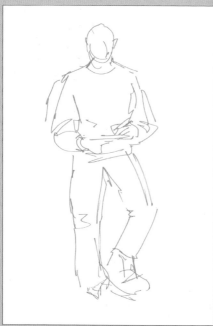

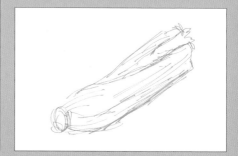

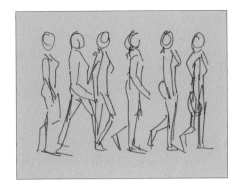

Action Drawing

Action drawing is closely linked to its gestural cousin, though as the name suggests, it focuses on subjects that are moving. The use of flowing lines and the search for the subject's essence remain the same. Ask a friend to model for you by walking around the room, pausing occasionally for 10 to 30 seconds to allow you to capture the dynamism expressed. Practise these action drawings in train stations, busy streets, coffee shops, zoos. For a quieter session, draw your non-drawing hand as it moves and twirls round in space. Or even draw what you're watching on television.

Drawing vs. Sketching

The different approach used in both gesture and action drawing points to the general difference between sketching and drawing. Sketching is thought of as more instinctive, rough and general, whereas drawing is more considered, neat and specific. They are not mutually exclusive, however, and should be thought of as two sides of the same coin. The one can influence the other, and by practising both you will add to your understanding and increase your appreciation of the world around you and your depictions of it.

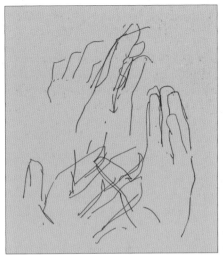

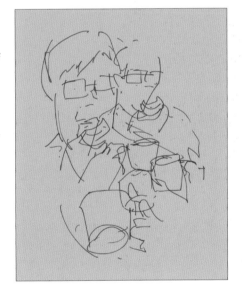

TRY THIS . . .

Time your gesture and action drawings with a watch or mobile phone, 10 to 30 seconds max. Knowing that you have a fixed time limit will focus you on the job at hand.

Starting Again

It is part of their myth that artists must suffer. The well-documented inner turmoil of Caravaggio, Van Gogh and Munch, for example, adds a dash of romance to their mysterious greatness. And improved technology now allows us to see the process that went into the making of many great works of art, a process often beset by various issues, struggles, workings and reworkings. To quote James Joyce, 'a man's errors are his portals to discovery'. When (not if) you make mistakes as you draw, don't get upset, don't rage against the unfairness of life: embrace your fallibility and move on.

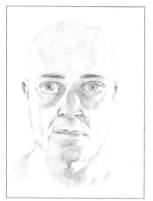

This drawing was originally done in light pencil and now seems a bit lifeless.

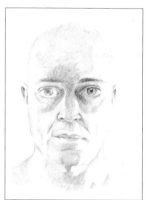

The left eye is first reworked with a greater detail and depth.

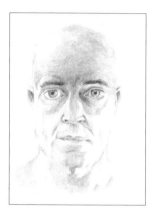

The head follows. The pencil describes the texture of the skin and is kept fluid.

A drawing tells at least two stories: the story of its subject and how it looked; and the story of the artist and how he or she came to draw the subject. There are traces left behind of both subject and artist as they grope towards and finally find one another. Errors, misjudgements and mistakes will likely pepper that journey, so if you end up with a drawing you aren't happy with, avoid the temptation to discard it. All drawings plot your progress, and you can even revisit the scene of the original crime and give it another go.

Divine Damage

Just as you started and finished the drawing, so you can restart and refinish, as many times as you wish. Pencil drawings are easier to revisit thanks to the rubber, though pen drawings can be similarly revised with judicious use of white paint or chalk. The resulting image will take the original drawing to a new level of potential and mystery. 'Divine damage' is the term given to the ghosts and echoes of the previous drawings that lie under the current layer. These remnants document your relationship not just with the subject, but with the drawing itself.

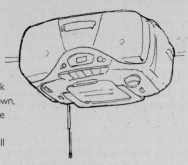

Keep abreast of your mistakes by taking a step back every now and then. Hold your drawing upside down, or see it reflected in a mirror. By slightly altering the context of your work, and giving it an alternative frame to the one you've been used to, mistakes will pop out.

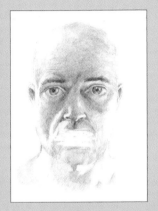

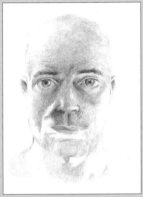

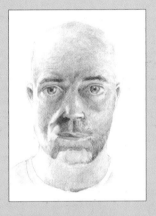

Parts of the original are revised with a rubber as the new drawing begins to take shape.

The mouth is redrawn, and a bit of extra stubble adds a little more character.

A denser beard and areas of shading create more three-dimensionality and presence.

The steps above document the rescue of an old drawing. The original was made about seven years prior, and was one of a series of self-portraits I did every night for a month. Having reworked it, the final image contains more information and shows a good level of improvement over the intervening seven years. The head seems more solid, and there's a greater resolution to the image as a whole. That's not to say I won't revise it in a few more years . . .

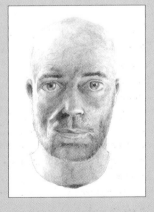

The viewer's eye is focused on the face by the lack of any background or clothing details.

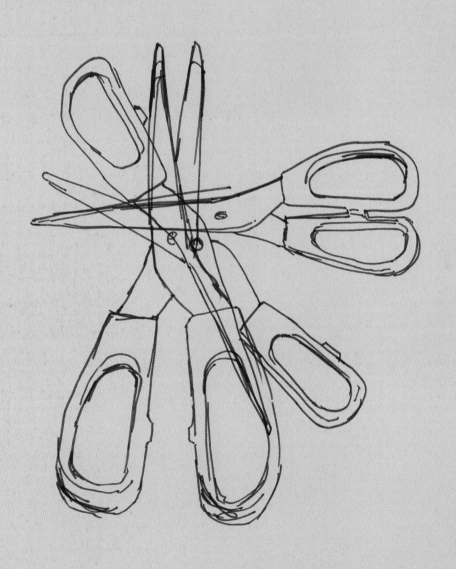

Loosening Up

As a musician must practise scales and arpeggios, or as an athlete must stretch and limber up, so these drills will help relax tense artistic fingers, soothe addled eyes and calm fried brains. Drawing is, in some ways, a restful, satisfying way of looking at the world around you that opens up new perspectives. These short, easy exercises should go some way towards getting you in the mood. You may find the rules restrictive – that's the point, as rules help focus you on the job at hand. For the moment, forget about communication or expression, and just enjoy looking and learning. It's worthwhile to remember these drills, as they will come in handy at whatever stage you get to in your drawing career.

Lines and Circles

Start with the basics. Lines and circles (and their associated variations) make up the fundamentals of how the visible world reveals itself to us. Drawing them over and over will help your hand and brain get used to the rhythms involved.

This exercise may prove to be harder than it looks. Bear in mind that it aims to equip you with greater confidence when it comes to making the first marks on your piece of paper. Starting simply is a way of learning faster. By drawing a series of straight lines, circles, spirals and ovals, we can soon get a feel for the medium in our hand and the relationship between the eye, the brain and the hand. Keep your pen or pencil moving and your hand fluid and supple. Don't cramp yourself with worry, and don't spend too long on each form. This exercise is continued and developed on page 66, where more weight is added.

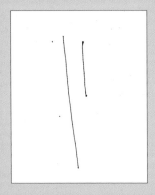

Draw two dots on the paper and connect with a straight(ish) line.

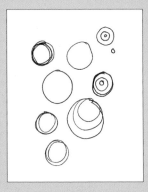

Draw a series of circles. Keep the pen moving, and correct as you go.

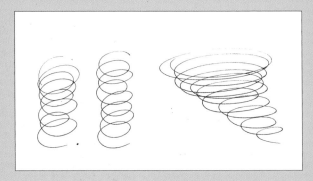

Holding your pen, twirl your hand around and around from the wrist, lower it to your paper, and draw a series of spirals.

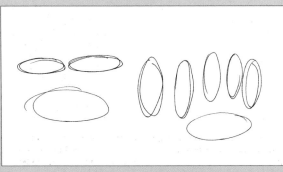

Draw oval shapes of various widths and lengths. Keep your movement light and fluid.

Doodling

On the phone, during a meeting or while waiting – the doodle comes into its own when we are in a kind of limbo between being present and being 'somewhere else'. That is why it's a great loosening-up exercise – the pressure's off and you can just take a line for a walk, wherever you want, without the need to draw something and have it look convincing, or even good. It's just your hand and your imagination.

Method

Take a piece of paper and any kind of pen. Draw something – a box, a tree, your cat, your mother – anything. Take it as far as you wish. Introduce a new medium – pencil, pastel, charcoal. Don't be afraid to leave it alone once you've had enough, but go back and continue working on it later. Over a period of time – a day, a week – you should have a record of apparently mindless drawing activity that may very well start to make some kind of sense (or not). You'll have generated a series of shapes, forms and images that act as a kind of portal into your own inner creativity and should increase your confidence in applying marks to paper.

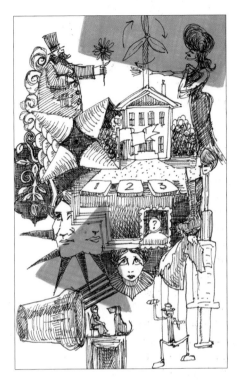

Doodles can be fun to draw, especially since the pressure is off. Weird situations can lead to even weirder ones.

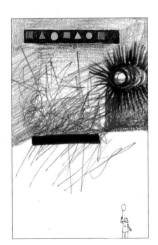

Use doodles to discover the range of possibilities for different media . . .

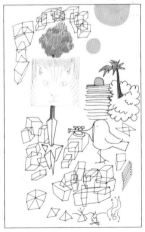

. . . or mix the abstract and figurative, as well as play around with different drawing styles.

Turning the Paper Off

This could almost qualify as a party game as much as an aid to help you learn more about the drawing process. Indeed, the first time I ever tried this was with a group of friends at about three in the morning after a few glasses of the proverbial sherry. You'll be drawing what is in front of you, but you must not look at the paper. Keep your focus on the subject and you may be surprised, dismayed or delighted by the results. Feel with your eyes and respond with the pencil.

Method

You'll only need one implement to draw with; take as long as you wish with each drawing. Start anywhere on the page, and try to let your hand and eye become one and the same. Don't go too fast. Draw as much of the outline and important details of your subject as you can – the cut-off point will probably come when you can no longer resist the temptation to look at the paper. Some of the marks you've made may seem absurdly placed, while others will be pretty spot-on. The final drawing is secondary to the process that got you there in the first place.

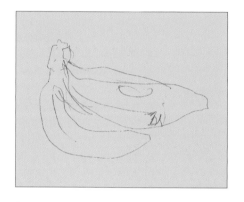

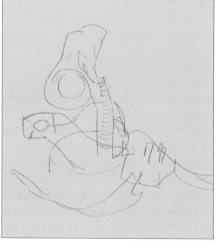

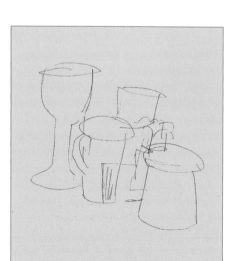

From the top, a bunch of bananas, a desk lamp and an arrangement of mugs and glasses. The line quality is totally different from that of my usual drawings – it's a lot freer and more playful.

Turning Your Eyes Off

This is an exercise that encourages both looking and remembering, and will help you realise the importance of both. Normally when we draw, our eyes dance between the subject and the paper. If the gap between the two gets too long, we start to forget some of the visual information. Here, the time for looking at the subject is cut, so you'll have to rely on memory to complete the picture. You should find that, once you've gone as far as your memory will allow, your understanding of the form takes over.

Method

Choose a subject and look at it. Think about its shape and angles, and notice any small detail that will help you root your drawing in the real world. Then, either turn away from it or place the subject somewhere it cannot be seen. Commit your memory to paper, working quickly and economically. The lines you remember best will doubtless be the strongest; as you begin to forget, the marks will be less convincing.

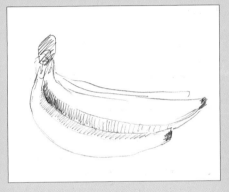

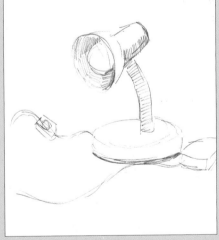

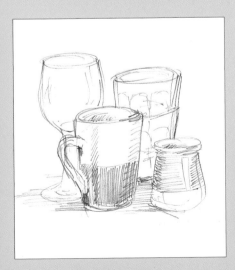

These examples feature the same subjects as on the previous page. The imagination starts to take over as the memory fades, and you look more to the drawing to help you along.

Drawing and Feeling

One reason to draw is to renew how you relate to what's around you. It's a tactile, sensual world, and the exercise here tries to get you to open yourself up to that. The aim is to draw with your eyes closed, using your free hand to feel around the subject. Your focus should not be on making a drawing that looks like your subject. It's more about creating a dialogue between the look and the feel of a given object and making a series of interesting marks that are inspired by the physical world.

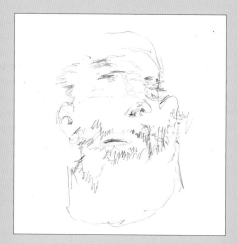

Method

A good subject for this exercise is your own head, as it is inevitably full of different textures and surfaces (it's also immediately accessible). You can also try drawing and feeling a range of fruit and vegetables. Just use pencils, and arrange a few of them so they're near to you, then close your eyes. Feel your way around your subject and try to communicate your impressions onto paper. Use the full variety of marks that a pencil gives you – soft and hard, clean and smudgy. Don't look at the paper until you've finished. What you'll end up with may look like nothing at all; reflect instead on the sensations you were feeling with one hand and describing with the other. In later drawings, made in a more typical way, use what you found here. Thinking about the physical nature of your subject will help you draw with increased sensitivity and awareness.

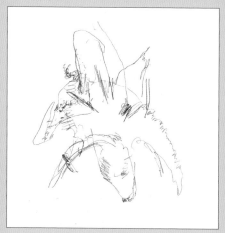

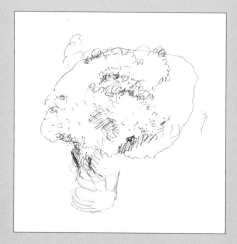

From the top: a self-portrait; a semi-peeled banana; and a head of broccoli. Limiting yourself to pencil will let you fully explore each subject's sensitivity and the range of possible marks.

Windshield Wipers

Here is another exercise to highlight the relationship between seeing and drawing as the line of your pencil receives a constant flow of information from your eyes. The movement of your gaze from subject to paper should be rapid and sustained – hence the exercise's name – and you should keep your pencil moving. As you continue to draw, you may find it hard to keep your eyes moving constantly; try putting some brisk music on in the background whose rhythm you can match.

Method

The only movement necessary here is that of your eyes, so position yourself and your paper sufficiently close to your subject to keep head jerks to a minimum. Start to draw, and keep feeding the marks you make with information from your eyes. You'll probably find your relationship with the subject seems more intense and more frenetic than usual – in a sense it is. Maintain the movement of both eye and hand at a constant pace, and don't bother trying to correct mistakes, as this will slow the process down.

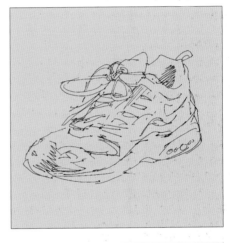

A trainer, a pot of pencils and the head of a thistle. A few marks are fed by a quick glance back to the subject – a process repeated over and over.

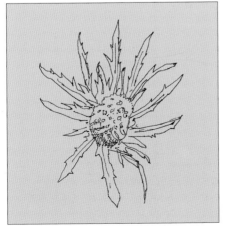

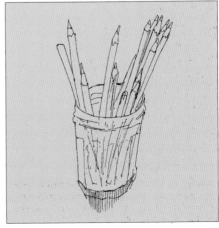

Two-Handed

It may sound like a recipe for disaster, but this exercise, in which you'll draw an object using two hands at the same time, will hopefully shed some light on what is involved when drawing form. Using both your left and right hands to draw a single picture, you'll be constantly made aware of the two sides of your subject, rather than just describing it with a single outline. In a way it feels like throwing clay on a potter's wheel, with both hands engaged in bringing something to life.

Method

Choose a simple object to draw. If it's too symmetrical, the challenge will be too easy – choose something with a few wobbles and kinks – an old building, a jug or a pile of clothes, for example. Take a pen or pencil in one hand, another in the other. Let them begin on the same starting point on the paper, then slowly move both around, creating an outline of the fullest shape you can see. You will become aware of the three-dimensionality of your object as both hands engage in trying to depict it. Then go back and fill in more detail, using the same two-handed method as you go. You'll notice the difference in the quality of your marks as your stronger hand will perform 'better'. Don't be deterred by this; instead focus on the fullness and unity of each shape as you work your way around.

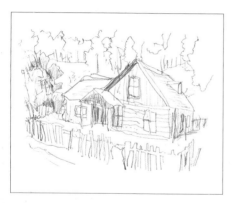

An old house, a jug and a pile of clothes. While none of these drawings is particularly accurate, creating them revealed much about depicting the fullness of form.

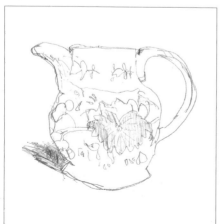

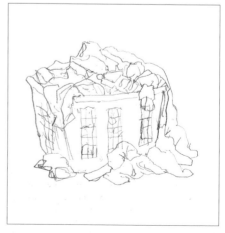

The Continuous Line

This exercise takes Klee's idea of a drawing as 'taking a line for a walk' to its logical conclusion: your pen or pencil must not leave the paper at all until you've finished. While it can be fun to the point of being maddeningly frustrating, think about the marks you're making as you progress. In some ways, drawing is a series of decisions regarding what goes where; think about your decisions here and what happens as a result.

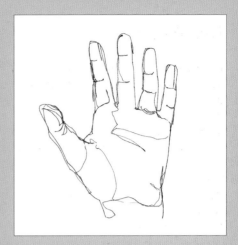

Method

Choose something to draw – your hand, a chair, a cup, whatever. Spend 30 seconds or so looking at its shape, angles and weight. Then start to draw without taking the pen or pencil off the paper. Don't spend too long on it or frustration may get the better of you, and don't worry too much about the accuracy of your drawing. Concentrate on where you are taking the line, and bear in mind that even drawing lines where there shouldn't be lines could make for a more interesting picture in the end.

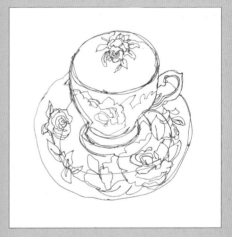

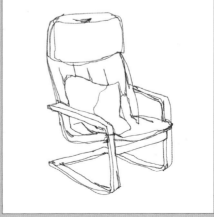

All of these examples have a curious energy that comes from the pen's constant engagement with the paper. A single line has been arranged in such a way as to depict these everyday objects.

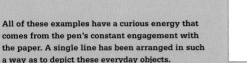

Added Length

By making drawings using unfamiliar methods, we not only discover new ways of working, but also see the more usual in a new light. Adding extra length to the shaft of your pencil will pose new challenges as you try to exert the same level of control over something much more unwieldy and foreign-feeling. As discussed already on pages 30 to 31, you can master the direction and flow of your drawing much better the closer you hold your pencil to its point. Relinquish control and instead create and investigate a whole new range of more abstract marks.

Method

Tape a pencil to a 30-centimetre (12-in) stick or ruler. Make sure it's secure. Decide to either place your paper on the floor, rest it on an easel or fix it to the wall. Select your subject, then make a series of drawings. Initially, hold the stick close to the pencil point, then increase the distance between the point and your hand. You can even 'super-size' your stick – add another foot and repeat the process. The drawings you make will be full of surprises as you learn that stepping out of your comfort zone can yield some interesting results. The exercise should also encourage you to see the drawing as a unit rather than just focusing on one small area at a time.

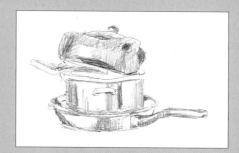

Near

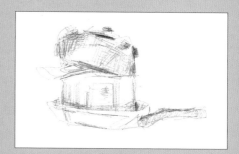

Midway

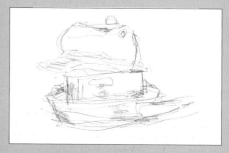

Far

The same group of pots and pans drawn with a pencil held at different lengths. Notice how the bottom image is no less interesting than the top (perhaps even more so), despite the loss of control over the drawing medium.

Layering Drawings

Three drawings of the same subject, all made on the same piece of paper on the same day. Going over a drawing may seem like a kind of art crime, especially if you think it's any good. But by adding layers of vision as time goes on, the resulting drawing will indicate a unity and an understanding of form that might have been missed by just doing one on its own. Move fluidly, with conviction, and without hesitation. The final picture will tell the story of its creation and your role in it.

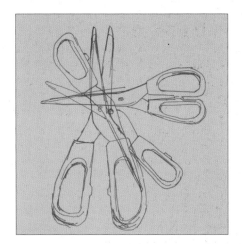

Method

Once you have chosen your subject, make your first drawing. Using either the same or a different medium, later in the day revisit the paper and add another layer. The fact that the pure white surface of the paper has already been disrupted by the first drawing should pose a few challenges. You must concentrate on the job at hand, though; a challenge that will itself force you to look harder. Later still, add another drawing, another layer. Alter your point of view with each layer – look down on your subject, up at it, from far away, from up close.

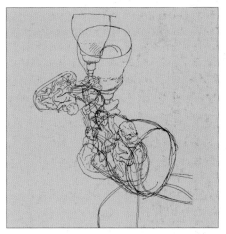

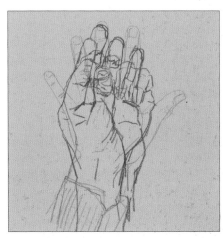

Drawing on top of something else really forces you to look at your subject carefully, as you have to find your way not only across the paper but also through the lines of the previous work.

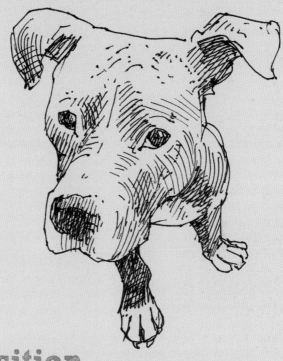

Composition

We're now ready to start looking at some of the key themes that are involved in the drawing process. The first is composition. We need to take into account the bones of the picture: what forms we are depicting; what we are leaving out; and how each separate element relates to the others. Certain standards used by artists for centuries will help you explore the possibilities for your final designs and make you aware of what makes for a harmonious picture. Remember the experience of the viewer also as they look at the final drawing.

Shapes

One way of seeing the world around us is in terms of geometry. Take your eyes away from this page for a moment and look at your surroundings – the different forms and shapes that make up where you are, such as windows, chairs, tables, buildings, other people and nature. So much can be broken down into separate constituent, regular-shaped parts. This way of seeing can be really useful when learning to draw; squares, rectangles, triangles and circles are so familiar that if you see them in the things you draw, it will help your powers of observation. You can also start to fill out your composition by thinking about the way different shapes relate to each other.

Becoming Solid

Returning to page 54, let's develop the lines and circles into something a little weightier. These exercises will help add weight to your shapes as you welcome them into the third dimension. Horizontal lines will slant off at an angle (unless the shape sits at eye level). By accurately depicting the angle, each shape will start to rise up from the paper. Vertical lines should always stay vertical. When objects start receding into the distance, as they tend to do, you'll need to start using perspective, details of which will come later in this section.

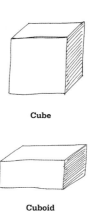

Cube

Cuboid

Draw a simple shape first – a square, rectangle, oval, curve or triangle. The addition of straight lines as shown, coming from various points of the shape, creates a sense of solidity. A few lines of shading help them along too.

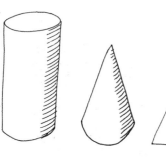

Cylinder   **Cone**   **Pyramid**

Cubism

Cubism was an art movement of the early 20th century that reversed the ideas illustrated here. Taking their lead from Cézanne and African and Iberian tribal art, Picasso and Braque (among others) reduced their subjects back to their component shapes. These simple shapes were then arranged on the canvas, following the essential form of their subject, but adding new points of view and ways of seeing. By turning the world into a series of interpenetrating solids, they set the evolution of art onto a new trajectory.

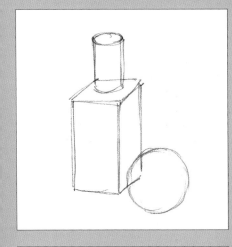

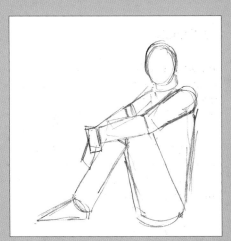

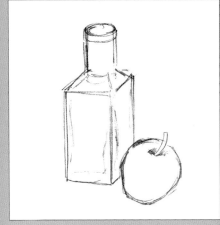

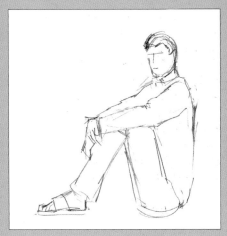

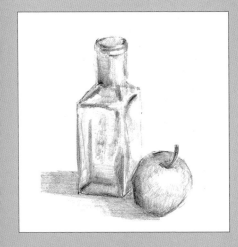

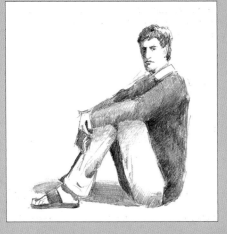

Some Rules of Composition

As much as art may be about freedom of expression and a world without boundaries, there are nevertheless valuable lessons and rules about how the eye reads a picture, something mentioned already on page 39. Once learned, you are of course free to break these, but for the beginner it is worthwhile familiarising yourself with a few tried and tested methods of creating a pleasing final picture. Remember that the rules featured here are not a wholly exact science, and your own intuition must also play a part in composing your picture.

The Golden Section

Alternately known as the Golden Mean or Phi, and closely connected to the Fibonacci sequence, the Golden Section is a ratio between length and width that is widely considered to be the most aesthetically pleasing. It is found in seashells, pine cones, hurricanes and galaxies, and has been exploited by designers of cars, credit cards and chocolate bars. The ratio is 6⅜:10, or approximately 1.61803. By dividing your paper along these lines, you can reach a point where it is thought to be most appropriate to place your primary object of focus.

The Rule of Thirds

If the Golden Section has indeed blinded you with science, fear not. A much simpler, user-friendly version draws on similar theories and yields similar, though less mathematically

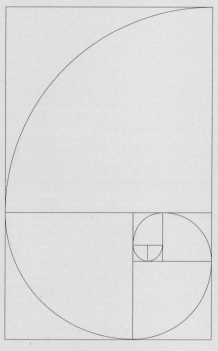

First, draw two equally sized squares, one on top of the other.

Turn them 90 degrees. Draw another square on top whose sides are equal to the combined length of the two smaller squares.

Repeat the process a number of times. Starting at the first square, draw an arc from one corner to the other. Repeat this through all the squares. The centre of the resulting spiral is an ideal focal point.

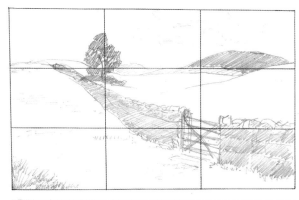

The line of background hills roughly lies across the top third, and the gate is placed in the lower-right intersection, echoing the tree at the upper left of the paper.

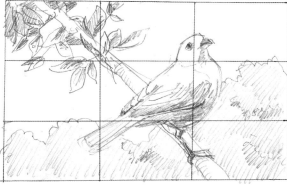

While the distant foliage falls from the upper to the lower third, the bird sits on the lower-right intersection, while some detailed leaves populate the top-left box.

robust, results. Used in photography and filmmaking as well as fine art, the rule of thirds imagines a grid of nine equally shaped squares or rectangles dividing up the picture plane. Any points of interest should be placed at the intersections (also known as power points or crash points) of the guidelines. It is argued that this makes for a more engaging composition than one that, for example, places your focal point in the centre. The rule of thirds creates rhythms within the picture as certain areas work in relation to others. A typical example is a landscape in which two-thirds of the picture is earth while the remaining third is sky. The rule of thirds also keeps the main subject away from the picture edges and adds a certain balance and harmony to your picture.

TRY THIS . . .

Play around with the rule of thirds. Draw out your nine squares or rectangles in pen, then in pencil lightly draw on top of the grid, mapping where different elements might be placed. You might like to try cutting out the elements and moving them around, leaving them at certain crash points and considering which works better.

Also, when you're watching a film or TV, or looking through a newspaper or magazine, consider how the pictures have been composed. Where do the main characters or points of interest fit within the larger frame?

Distance

If you want your drawing to act as a kind of window into another world beyond the four corners of your piece of paper, it helps to create a sense of depth. Done well, it can tell your viewer a whole new story as you communicate distance and use certain devices to emphasise foreground, background and the bits in between. Perspective is discussed over the next few pages, but first let's look at arrangement and tone.

Arrangement

Your composition can be enlivened if certain elements overlap. Arranging each separate object in a line parallel to where you're sitting will make for a static, flat picture. Bring some to the front, however, while leaving others behind, and you'll animate your group. Each separate form will feed into and out of the next, making for a more engaging final drawing.

Balancing your layout results in a greater overall harmony. Grouping together all the large or dark elements will overload that area, leaving the rest of the drawing fighting a losing battle. Punctuate the whole scene with moments of interest, creating relationships between those objects and the spaces they occupy.

Aerial Perspective

The human eye does not see all objects with the same degree of clarity – a phenomenon known as aerial perspective. Things that are further away are hazier and softer than the sharply focused objects lying under your nose. Imagine looking into the far distance on a hot, sunny day: the hills in the distance are almost invisible, whereas you can make out each individual leaf on the tree next to you. So by varying the tonal values of each separate element, increasing or decreasing the amount of detail and changing the weight of your media, you should find that your drawing comes alive with a sense of rhythm and recession. This rule applies to scenes with both deep and shallow depths of field, as the still life on the right demonstrates.

1   This still life was made up of various objects lying around the house. They were grouped dynamically, with some further away than others and many forms overlapping. The white background makes the group easier to see.

2   Having drawn out the still life as a series of outlines with a medium-soft pencil, I used a slightly harder pencil to shade in areas of the back bottle. This hardness is useful when drawing material like glass. The shading was kept light, bearing in mind aerial perspective.

3   I then worked on the next bottle. Because it was brown, the contrast with what was behind it was more noticeable – a useful aid to achieving a greater sense of depth. The bristles of the brush were then drawn, with particular focus on the way the light created a variety of tonal values.

TRY THIS . . .

Draw three squares, one slightly behind the other and leading away from you. Draw them all using the same medium. Then choose a thick pen for the nearest one, a finer one for the next and a sharp pencil for the square farthest away. See the difference? By using well-selected materials you immediately create greater depth.

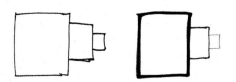

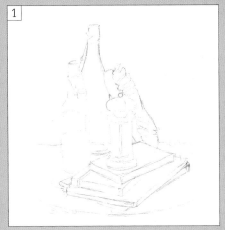

1

2

3
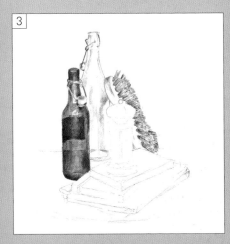

4
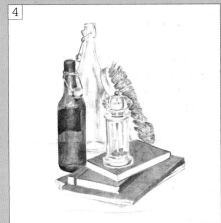

5
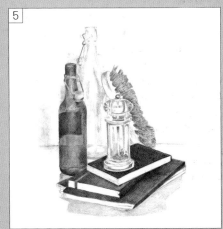

4 The picture starts to come to life as the other objects get filled in. The glass pepper mill was also drawn with a harder pencil, while the selection of sketchbooks was done with a softer pencil more suited to their dark covers.

5 As I finished, I worked over the book covers with harder strokes to bring them right out to the viewer. The back bottle was then very gently worked with a plastic rubber to lighten the detail even more and emphasise the contrast with the pepper mill at the front. The books' shadows help to bring the viewer into the picture and anchor the group to its surroundings.

Negative Space

Space is all round us: it lies between the tiniest cracks and fills the biggest chasms. But what does it actually look like? One way of approaching a drawing is to focus not on the subject, but on the space around it.

Often when we draw, we focus all our energy on capturing the subject alone. In reality, though, the subject occupies its own position within three dimensions. The following exercise encourages you to try to look at what lies between the gaps that, in their own way, describe the subject just as effectively. This space is known as 'negative space'. It is also an exercise that aims to free you from drawing what you think you know about your subject and instead focus on what your eyes are actually telling you.

The use of negative space has informed the work of some of the most famous artists, musicians, writers and even schools of thought in history. Pauses in a theatrical production can reveal as much as the dialogue; the empty gaps between the panels of a comic strip are the magical bits where readers make their own connections between what came before and what comes after; much of Japanese art and design is grounded in a balance between the 'shown' and the 'unshown'.

Vase or Face?

During the course of his work into human perception, Danish psychologist Edgar Rubin (1886–1951) developed a series of optical illusions that play with the notion of what is and isn't there. The famous Rubin Vase is both a vase against a plain background and two people facing each other in profile. The lines describing the forms are identical; the interpretation lies with the viewer.

TRY THIS . . .

A simple way to start is to look at the word 'DRAW' written in bold capital letters. Instead of focusing on each individual letter in its entirety, just notice the spaces formed within them – two differently sized semicircles in the 'D' and the 'R' and a triangle in the 'A'. Using your sketch pad, draw out these shapes as they appear in the word, focusing on their form and where each sits in relation to the other.

Next, draw in the rest of the letters and see how even, or otherwise, your resulting letters are. Don't worry if they're not perfect – the main thing is to focus on the space you'd otherwise ignore. When you get ready to draw in the future, bear in mind how the space around your subject can help you plot your composition.

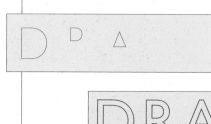

Exercise

You'll need a sharp HB pencil, a rubber and something to draw (ideally something with strong, simple shapes). If you can, set your subject in front of a plain piece of card or cloth – this will make the shapes stand out more clearly. You may also want a softer pencil for shading the background.

Equipment

- HB pencil
- 3B pencil
- Rubber

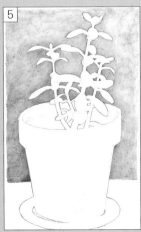

[1] Before you draw, look at your subject for a while. Think about its overall shape, and how that will fit onto your paper. Familiarise yourself with the spaces it describes, and the space that describes it. Then draw your first space.

[2] In relation to that space, draw more. Keep looking at the subject. This is not a test – relax and enjoy the simple relationship between you and space.

[3] Adapt and adjust the lines you've drawn as necessary. Don't be spooked by mistakes – that's what your rubber is for.

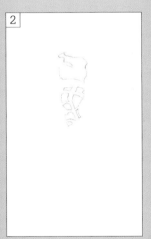

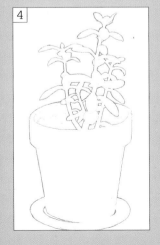

[4] You can make darker, more certain lines once you're confident they're in the right place. It may feel like you're carving the subject out of space and into your drawing.

[5] By shading some of the background, the plant is thrust forward.

One-Point Perspective

Linear perspective is the scheme whereby objects appear smaller and closer together the further away they are. In very early art, the size of an individual object would reflect its thematic importance or status. Only during the Renaissance in Italy did perspective really come into its own (though in fact it had been mulled over and discussed at length for centuries before). Remember that perspective is a device, not a hard set of rules that must be strictly adhered to. It's a theory that has withstood the ravages of time and as such must be understood. But, ultimately, draw only with an awareness of the effects of perspective – why the shapes are receding, why they are getting closer together – rather than making pictures that are loaded with so much mathematical precision that anything else of interest takes a back seat.

Useful Terms

First, it'll be useful to introduce some terms relating to perspective.

Picture Plane: The flat surface of your drawing that can be imagined as a pane of glass through which you and your viewer are looking.

Field of View: The full extent of what you can see at any given moment.

Eye Level: Looking straight ahead of you, your eye level is the height at which you observe the subject, like your own personal horizon.

Converging Lines: Lines that are parallel in reality appear to converge when seen from a distance.

Vanishing Point: The point at which the converging lines meet.

All lines appear to lead to and from this one spot, the vanishing point, on the horizon.

These converging railway tracks look like they meet, when we know in real life they never touch.

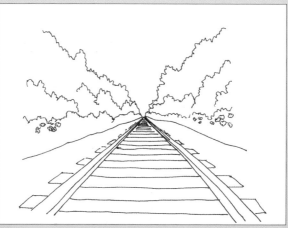

This eye level is slightly higher than the horizon, which means the tracks can be looked down on and the trees looked up at.

The four corners of this drawing form the extent of the picture plane.

One-Point Perspective

The simplest form of perspective is one- (or single-) point perspective. Any horizontal or vertical lines that run parallel to your field of vision will remain parallel. Any lines that lead away from your field of vision, however, will converge as they recede.

Look at the example below. Draw a straight line in your sketch pad and mark a vanishing point on it. Then draw a square nearby. Now draw a series of lines from each of the square's corners to the vanishing point. Drawing a horizontal and adjoining vertical line anywhere within that range of vision will give you a nicely receding block. Repeat the exercise using different shapes – you'll discover any number of forms that all sit in perfect relation to each other within the picture plane.

> ## TRY THIS . . .

Take a cereal box and place it in front of you. Observe and draw it from different angles, bearing in mind one-point perspective. See how the vertical lines will always remain vertical, but the lines receding away from you will start to converge.

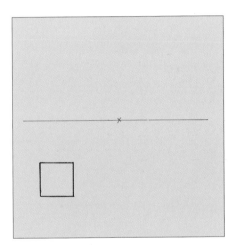

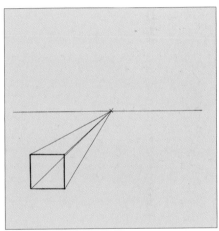

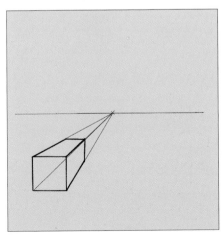

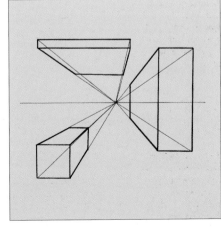

Extra Perspective

To make things more interesting, there's more to perspective than just one-point. When you can see more than one set of lines leading away from you (in other words, lines at different angles), more vanishing points are required, creating two-point, three-point and even multipoint perspective.

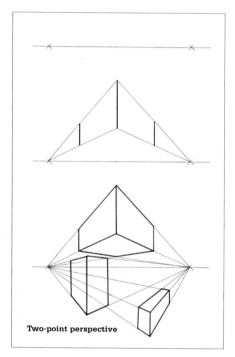

Two-point perspective

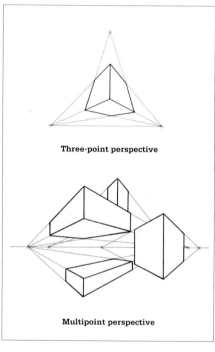

Three-point perspective

Multipoint perspective

Start with two vanishing points this time, then draw a straight line. Connect both ends to both points and the objects will soon take shape. A third vanishing point is used when looking up at or down on your final object, while many vanishing points create a network of separate units. Because they share the same horizon, however, the shapes still look spatially convincing.

Foreshortening

Foreshortening is a close relation of perspective, yet its rules are not as mathematically reasoned. It concerns the relation of an object to you, particularly when that object is seen at an angle. It almost plays tricks on you, as it goes against all common sense.

Hold this book out in front of you and at an angle. The form is foreshortened, as one part looks closer to you than the other. As discussed, perspective can help create a realistic impression. So what about when a more organic shape, such as a hand, is angled towards you? Trying to plot enough vanishing points and converging lines to convey it convincingly will only leave you thoroughly strung out. You must instead trust your eyes, forget everything you know about the three-dimensional world, and see the form as a two-dimensional object.

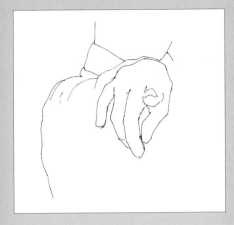

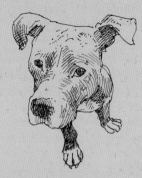

This dog may not look like it has much of a body and only two legs, but we can imagine the whole hound quite comfortably.

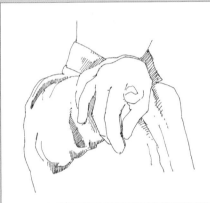

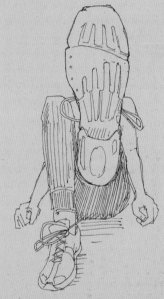

This drawing of someone raising their leg completely obliterates their torso and face. The focus is on the trainer sole.

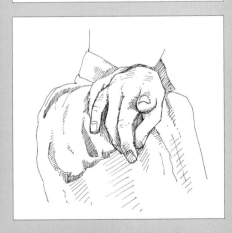

In this drawing of someone pointing at the viewer, the arm has been foreshortened behind an enlarged hand. Darker lines around the hand emphasise its presence.

TRY THIS . . .

Find a photograph of a foreshortened form. Look at it, then copy or trace it. Doing this will help you understand what is involved in bridging the gap between what your eyes see and what your brain knows.

Project: Landscape

Bringing together different elements to create an effective composition can be tricky. You need to consider the viewer's experience as well as your own, and how the eye will read the final drawing. Certain established methods have been discussed earlier in this chapter, such as contrasting foreground and background, the use of thirds, and perspective. This landscape project brings some of these methods together to encourage you to do the same.

Before you start your composition, take a walk with a camera (the one on your mobile phone will do). You don't need to be anywhere special – focus purely on how you frame what you see, and look for harmony. Take a sketch pad with you too, and create a visual record of anything you find interesting.

I took some photos and made a few sketches on a recent bicycle trip through the rolling countryside. Reviewing them later, I decided to draw these hay rolls in more detail at home. The rolls form a stark contrast to the gentle hills in the background, and I added a few more fence posts to take the eye further back. The amount of sky also meant that I could play around with the idea of negative space.

I decided pen was the ideal medium to convey the scratchy, linear forms of the hay and grass, with pencil for the sky for a much softer counterpoint.

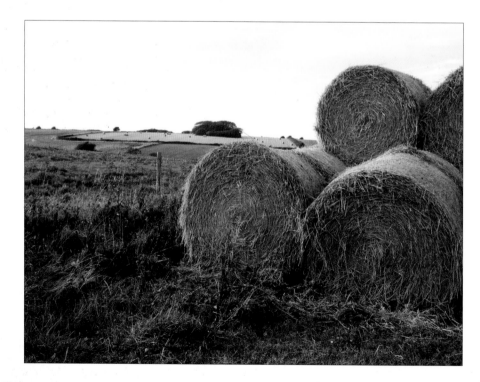

Exercise

Equipment
- Fibre-tip pens
  (0.4 and 0.05)
- HB pencil
- 3B pencil
- Rubber

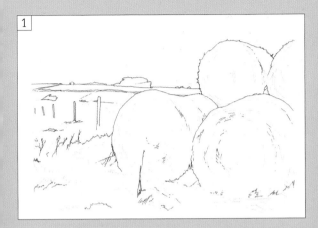

1 I went over the faintly sketched outline with the slightly thicker 0.4 fibre-tip pen to give the work some solidity and a kind of anchor.

2 Most of the remaining pen-work was done with the much finer 0.05, which allows for greater subtlety and variety. I started with the background and middle ground, remembering to keep the line relatively light and faint.

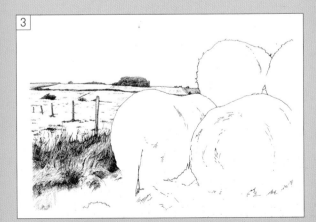

3 Moving onto the grass at the left, I picked out the denser areas with a greater number of pen strokes. I didn't want to copy the photo exactly – just to get a sense of the rhythms and textures.

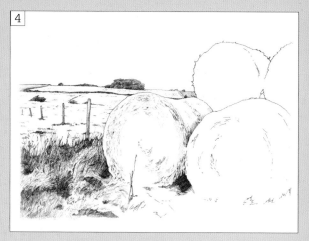

4 | I then started on the rolls. Drawing is like a journey of discovery; doing the fields first, then the grass, enabled me to start the rolls with more confidence.

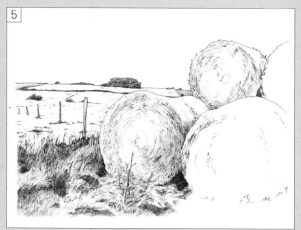

5 | As the work progresses, you become more comfortable with it. I tried half-closing my eyes to match the tonal variations of the photo. Let your pen dance over the paper.

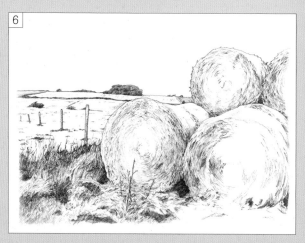

6 | Hay is probably not the easiest thing to draw, but you can go back and rework it until it feels right. The lines create tonal areas and suggest contours and form.

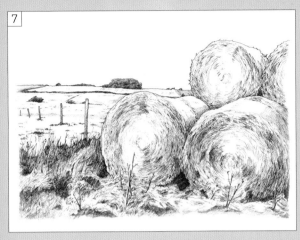

7 I added a few more grassy stalks to break up the foreground – another compositional device like the imaginary fence posts.

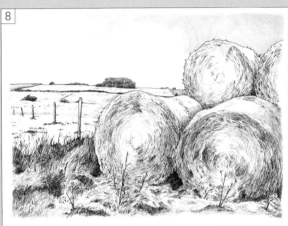

8 Once I was happy with the pen work, I turned to the sky. Light shading at first …

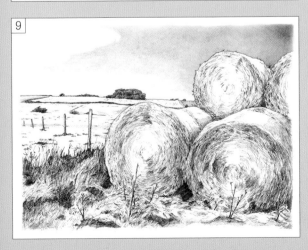

9 … moving to darker shading, which creates an atmosphere within the drawing that is absent from the photo. The change of medium contrasts nicely with the empty paper at the top left (the cloud), which balances the more defined hay rolls at the bottom right.

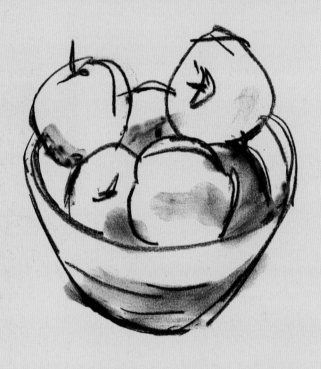

Line

Line is the most basic drawing technique. You can keep a drawing simple by describing your subject with the faintest of outlines. At the other end of the scale, multiple lines can be used to show a richness of depth, volume, substance and distance. The way line is handled can also speak volumes about the person behind the pen. This section serves as an introduction to what line offers and encourages you to find out how it can work for you.

Line Qualities

As already discussed, there's a wide range of materials out there to draw with, and most are designed to make lines. In particular, pens, pencils and coloured pencils are good for line work. Their versatility and sensitivity should be fully exploited, giving you the option to create drawings of real simplicity, intricate elegance, hard-edged brutality and all points in between. Having played around with each medium, you should be familiar with its style and texture; use this knowledge when selecting the one (or ones) that will be most appropriate for a particular drawing. Remember that the way you hold your material can have a huge impact on the marks you make.

Contour Drawing

A contour drawing is the most basic kind. You are essentially drawing the outline of the subject and any important details within it. As well as describing the basic form of your subject, the line you use can also convey the fall of light upon it, its texture, and also its spatial surroundings. By altering the thickness and the strength of your line, your drawing will appear more engaging and dynamic.

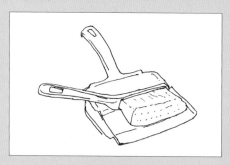

Pen outline: a basic line drawing conveying all information in a line of uniform width and depth.

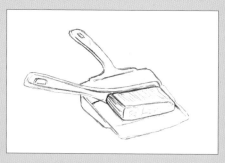

Mixed pencil outline: value can be suggested by different pencil grades.

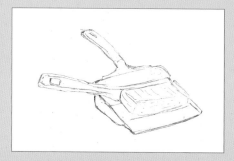

Pencil outline: pencil allows for a greater margin of error and a more sensitive line.

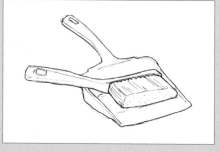

Mixed media outline: using different media adds interest and depth.

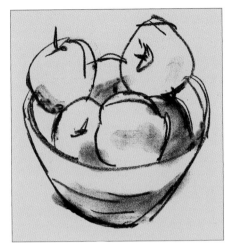

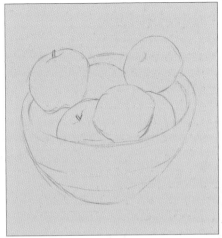

Mood

Varying the quality of the line will heighten the descriptive potential of your work. Atmosphere as well as appearance can be communicated by a sensitively drawn line, adding weight and interest to the final picture. Notice how the same bowl of fruit drawn in two different styles reflects different moods – the rougher, expressive charcoal on the left versus the calm coloured pencil on the right.

TRY THIS . . .

You may or may not prefer to listen to music when you draw. For this little exercise, put some music on and draw along with it. The subject is not as important as the lines you make in response to it – just abstract scribbles will do. Try to vary the music you hear, and let the mood of each piece determine how your lines turn out. Once completed, reflect on your results and what lessons you can take from them. Below are marks made when listening to (from left) classical, techno and funk.

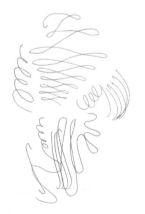

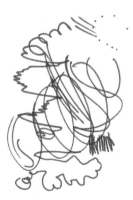

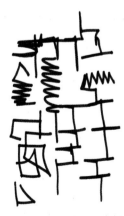

Multiple Lines

You can now start to investigate the full range of possibilities afforded by using more than one simple line. Activate your drawing with a series of outlines, rather than just one, or use multiple lines in what's known as a cross-contour drawing. Drawing with a series of lines as opposed to just one leads the eye around the form the lines describe, creating a sense of rhythm and giving the viewer more to engage with. More lines can also mean more potential for tonal value, expression, mood and energy.

Multiple Outlines

Loosen up your approach to the simple contour drawing with shorter, more fluid marks. Keep your hand moving as you describe the form, and allow your drawing tool to make mistakes. Any pressure to make the drawing as accurate as possible with just one line will ease and be replaced by a more spontaneous energy.

Cross Contours

As certain lines on a map describe terrain, cross contours travel across the form and plot the peaks and troughs. They can be drawn at any angle and work best when closely following the subject's individual topography. Each contour should be sympathetic to the subject as a whole. Use the play of light and dark on your subject to locate the shifts in angles, and draw them in accordingly. The one danger with such drawings is that they can look cold and mechanical, as if you've processed a digital wire-frame image. Use cross contours judiciously, therefore, or think about blending or erasing some of them before you finish.

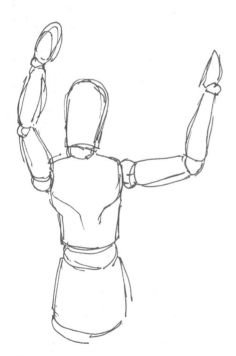

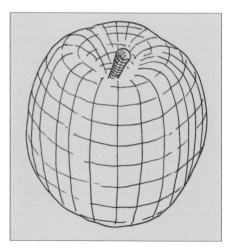

The various outlines add a sense of movement to this drawing of an artist's mannequin.

See how the gaps in some of the cross contours suggest the fall of light on this apple.

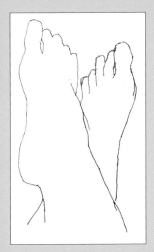

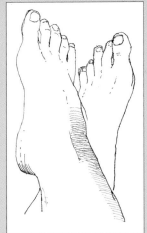

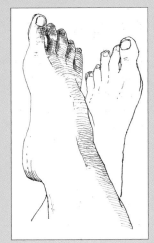

This series shows the development of a cross-contour drawing of my feet. Starting with a rough outline, the cross-contours then try to follow each foot around, describing the underlying structure as well as the fall of light. In darker sections, differently angled lines create more depth. Don't be tempted to cover your subject with cross-contours – give your drawing room to breathe.

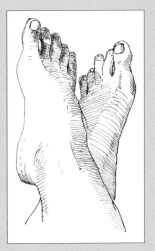

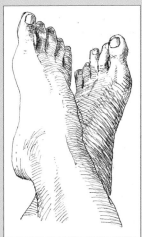

TRY THIS . . .

Heavy cotton or woolen clothing is ideal for initial cross-contour drawings, as the rows of fibres that make up the material are still evident. Loosely bundle up a thick sock, jumper or similar, set it in front of you, and light it well. Draw the outline, then observe how the direction of fibres makes up the individual folds.

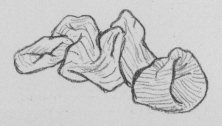

The Invisible Line

Making the first mark can often be the hardest part of the drawing process. You may well feel tense as the pressure to get it 'right' from the start mounts; make a mistake now and you may as well throw the picture in the bin. Well, maybe not, but one way of feeling your way into a drawing is to use invisible (or barely visible) lines and marks to help plot your way around both paper and subject.

Guidelines

When planning your composition, guidelines can be invaluable tools. Draw them faintly, and they will help you plot the separate elements and their relation to one another. Observe your subject closely and carefully, then use guidelines, made with equal care and precision, to start your drawing off by revealing the most essential forms. Guidelines can construct basic shapes, help you with perspective, and act as a kind of skeleton from which you can develop tone and colour. Once the drawing is finished, they can be erased or, more interestingly, incorporated into the final design to reveal more of the story of its creation.

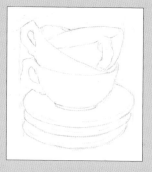

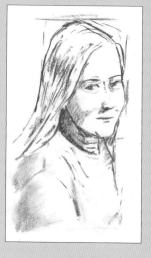

The space occupied by this setup of cups and saucers has been marked off with a series of faint lines . . .

. . . while marks roughly showing the form of the girl's skull underlie this charcoal portrait.

Guidelines were useful when drawing this seated self-portrait (right). The head, once drawn, acts as a basic sighting unit (see page 43), which is then marked off on the page. The width of the chair in relation to my crossed leg is also noted. Smaller marks, such as those describing the fall of the T-shirt sleeves, weren't actually there, but suit the feel of the final drawing.

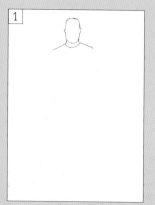

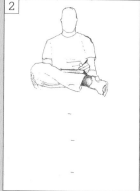

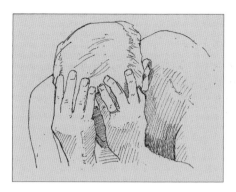

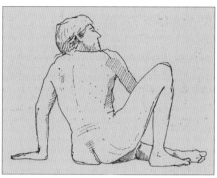

The combination of both barely there marks and the cross contours add life to this head and hand study . . .

. . . while the tiny dots that map this figure suggest the underlying anatomy too.

Mapping the Body

I often find when drawing a figure that even the slightest dot or line on the paper, made in relation to another dot or line I've already done, helps me map out that particular section before committing myself to something more resolved. By taking my pen to the area I want to go to, leaving a slight mark at the end point, it's like I'm familiarising myself with the journey I'm about to take. The body is often referred to, art historically at least, as a landscape whose dips and curves are like valleys and hills. Think about plotting your own subjects with these marks –

mostly tiny dots or ticks – and notice how, when left in, they add a subtle, exciting energy to your final drawings.

TRY THIS . . .

Plot the outline of an object in front of you using only a series of tiny dots or lines. Be as economical as you can – focus on the main nodes or corners. You should start to feel like you're drawing in space as you familiarise yourself with the form before committing any stronger lines to paper.

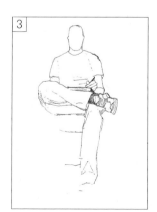

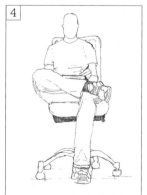

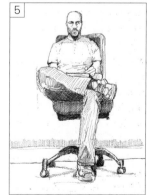

Project: Still Life

You should now have a good understanding of the potential of line. You can plot with it, plan ahead, and in doing so, make life easier for yourself. You can also investigate the full range of mark-making possibilities presented by each drawing tool, which in turn offers you a wealth of expression. This still-life project offers you an example of how the potential of line can be exploited for maximum effect.

Exercises such as the ones that make up the majority of this book can be practised using everyday objects that may be lying around and are easy to set up. To make a more detailed still life that you'll want to spend a bit more time with, it makes sense to choose objects that you find visually interesting. Maybe they're curiously shaped or have an exciting texture. Subjects may also be chosen because they have some kind of personal resonance for you – a favourite item of clothing or a childhood toy.

Anything that will keep you excited and focused is ideal. Remember to group your items dynamically by playing with depth, line and form, and also to consider your light source.

1 The group was sketched out in pencil. I realised the plant was going to be particularly tricky, so I made a few simplifications – I was happy to capture its essential form and not get too hung up on the smaller details.

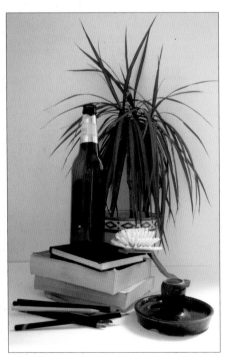

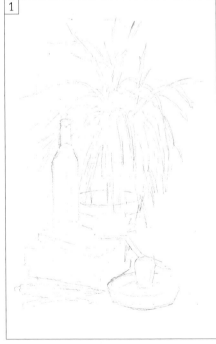

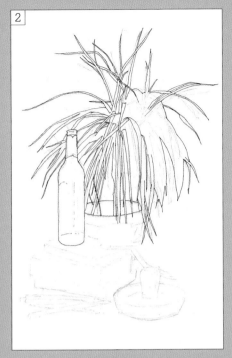

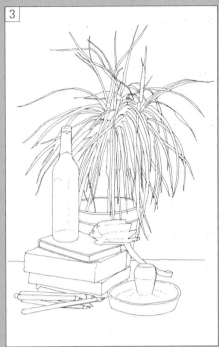

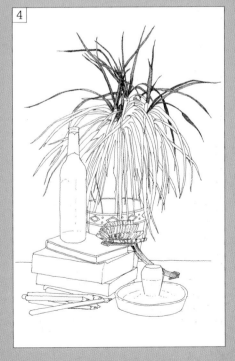

2 I then switched over to my main drawing medium, the 0.4 rollerball. The ink flows smoothly, and you can build up a variety of values with careful working of the line.

3 A few 'barely there' marks helped me plot some of the object forms (even though I'd roughed out the group in pencil) to give them greater energy.

4 I then erased the pencil to remove the excess noise and start with a clean page. Keeping the pen fluid, I started initially with the lightest area, the bristles of the brush. Looking back, maybe I went in a bit too hard. Then I started on the plant.

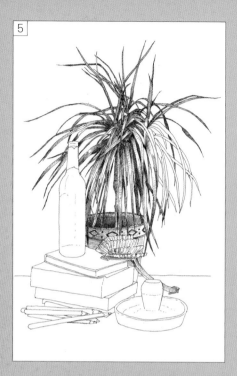

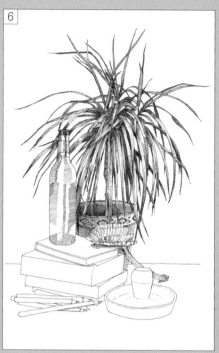

5   As time went on, I was silently cursing myself for choosing such a difficult plant! Still, I persisted, feeding the drawing with continual glances back at the group, working the darkest areas of shadow within the plant with heavier areas of pen.

6   Just as the cross-contours described the form of each leaf, the bottle was rendered with similarly descriptive lines. The reflections on the glass were worked on from the start.

7   Having worked the bottle, the solid black of the sketchbook underneath was then tackled with a series of closely interweaving lines.

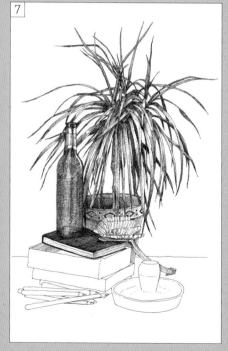

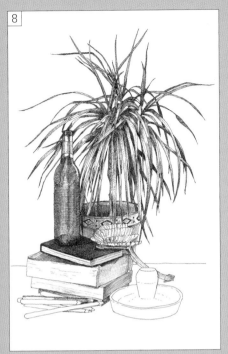

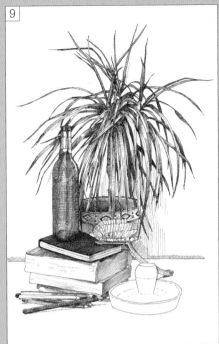

8 The softer book edges came as something of a welcome relief. The line was kept light and sensitive while still observing the effects of the soft daylight I was drawing in. I solidified the sketchbook cover by adding more lines, throwing the bottle and brush into starker relief.

9 After the pencils were shaded in, I drew a few suggestions of a shadow against the background to give the group a more physical context ...

10 ... and finished with the candle holder and some more vague shadows to anchor the drawing. A few more details were teased out later after I'd had a break from it, enabling me to look at the work with fresh eyes.

10

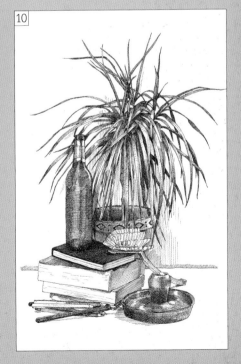

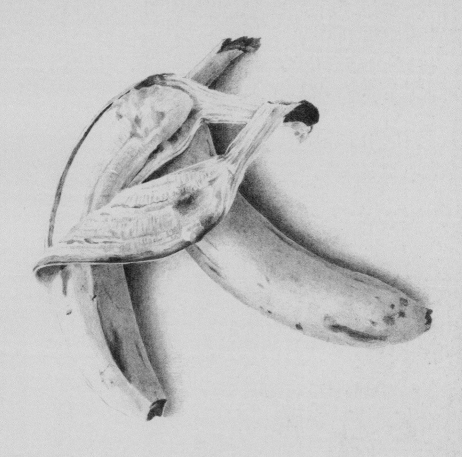

Value

Different values, be they shadows or highlights, will lift your subject off the two dimensions of your drawing surface, making it more three-dimensional and more realistic. Value is sometimes referred to as 'tone', and it is directly affected by the degree, direction and quality of light upon your subject. It is not just a question of light and dark, as the subject's colour also has a direct influence on the different tonal variations.

Light and Dark

Drawings are usually monochromatic affairs, depicting a world that is flush with colour. The challenge for an artist is how to bring the two together, and knowing which of the various methods of recreating value should be used.

Seeing Value

Your starting point for any successful value drawing is to try to see how the light describes an object. Hold this book up, then take stock of where the light is coming from. Are you by a window? Are you reading outside? Are you under a desk lamp, or in the blazing sunshine? Then notice how that light is falling on and around the book. In stronger light (especially artificial), you'll find that the contrasts between highlight and shadow are more pronounced. Softer, more ambient lighting gives values that have more in common with each other. If you can, alter your surroundings, repeat the exercise, and notice the changes.

The next stage is to think about those values in terms of black and white and the bits in between. In other words, discount the colour. Imagine taking a photograph of this book with a black-and-white camera: How will it come out? How sharp are the shadows? Where and how do the highlights fall? Alternately, take a sheet from the sketch pad and make a tube with it. One side will be darker than the other – how dark? And what about the inside of the tube?

Then look around you and focus on a more colourful object – what story is the light telling now? Reducing the world all around you to a palette of grey may not seem like an appealing exercise, but it will open your eyes to the huge array of subtleties afforded by light.

Chiaroscuro

The dramatic properties of light have been explored and exploited by artists over many centuries. This contrast between light and dark, also known as 'chiaroscuro', helps to create a convincing sense of space within the picture plane. Work by artists such as Leonardo (whose 'Study for the Head of the Virgin' is shown here on the right) and Vermeer was helped by their use of light as a key aid to modelling and capturing the form. In later works by painters like Caravaggio and Rembrandt, however, light assumes a more symbolic power and becomes as much a part of the subject as the things being depicted.

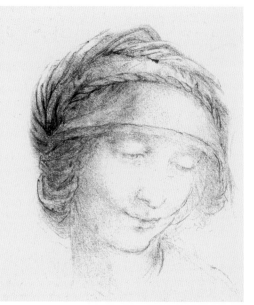

Techniques

As shown earlier, different drawing tools can produce very different effects, and each tool will similarly produce its own tone range and tonal characteristics. Familiarise yourself with these results and you'll be able to choose the right medium. Softer media like charcoal, pastel and pencil allow a much wider range than pen, for example, and by increasing the pressure you increase the variation. Don't feel limited to one medium per drawing – play around with what's available for full effect.

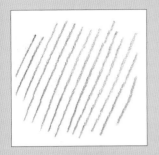

Hatching: A series of parallel lines drawn closer together for darker areas and further apart for lighter areas.

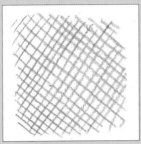

Cross-Hatching: Two layers of hatching going in different directions. The spaces between them determine the final value.

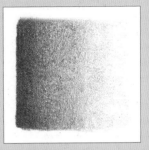

Shading: A light and fluid motion; the pressure eases as the pencil moves to the right.

Blending: Use a piece of tissue or a stump – available at most art shops – to soften the graphite.

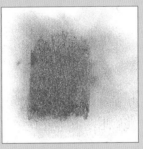

Smudging: Carefully use your finger to create a more expressive way of working with value.

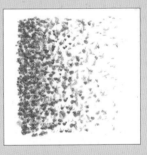

Stippling: A series of rapidly drawn dots, stippling is a more labour-intensive technique, but one that gives you texture and depth.

TRY THIS . . .

To focus your eyes on the monochrome world, look up sources on black-and-white photography. Try to imagine what colours each photographer was confronted with, and how light played its part in creating each image (though remember that the eye sees things differently from the camera). Many computers these days allow you to desaturate colour images (i.e., turn them black and white) – play around with a copy, then compare it to the original. Reflect on which colours become what values.

More Light and Dark

Given the complexity of how light behaves, it may surprise you to learn that, as an estimate, the human eye can generally only detect up to ten different shades of grey. It sounds improbable, but when working out a value scale (see below) the reality becomes only too clear. These separate tones are similar to the notes of a piano scale – both artists and musicians have a limited range with which to create a satisfying piece of work.

The Value Scale

Similar to the pencil familiarisation exercises on page 20, the value scale is a more structured introduction to the different shades between black and white. Starting at white, the amount of shading in each successive box increases until ultimately you get to black. This row of tonal values represents the full range, and is known in some quarters as 'full contrast', which is itself one kind of a 'key'. Depending on the subject and mood of your final drawing, you may want to limit yourself to just certain tones towards the high or low end (for softer drawings) or use the full range.

Outside In

Another possibility is to work from the edges out. In other words, study your subject and first identify the darkest shade – this will be rendered black in your picture. Then identify the lightest areas – these will be left blank. Then work back so any subsequent shades are always made in relation to those two extremes. Staying within the bounds of such opposites will heighten the drama of your work.

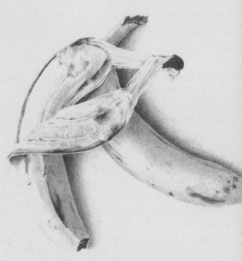

In this drawing, soft shadows gently elevate the bananas from the page and towards the viewer.

TRY THIS . . .

The best way of discovering more about different values is to practise. Take a sharp HB pencil and fill small areas of the page with various tones. Use swift, small circular or sideways movements and keep the pencil light in your fingers. Try to replicate the scale above by increasing the pressure of graphite on paper.

1

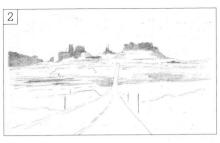

2

With the focus on value in this drawing, only the faintest outline was needed at the start.

The rock formations in the distance are drawn with a grainy, dry style of HB pencil . . .

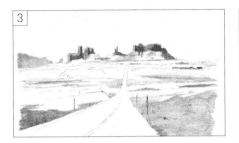

3

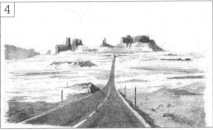

4

. . . which suits the dusty desert setting. The tones help capture the hazy, dusty heat.

As the drawing progresses, the value of the road and the line it makes connects us to the horizon.

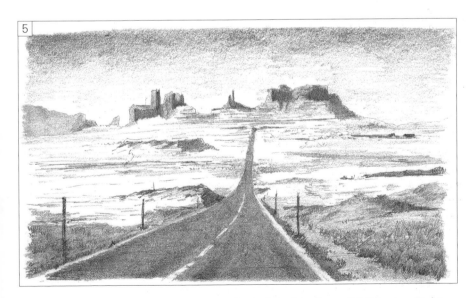

5

A gentle sky added at the end helps frame the scene. Remember to keep the pencil fluid to prevent bands appearing across your shading and fade the sky out as you reach the horizon.

Getting Lighter

When working with value, it's not just about what you put in but also what you bring out. A white sheet of paper immediately offers any artist a starting tone. However, this usual process can be reversed if you instead use a rubber as your principal drawing tool. Whether you work back into already-drawn areas or create lightness from a dark ground, new layers of interest will be added for both you and your viewer.

Drawing with Rubbers

Pity the poor rubber – forever associated with mistakes and trying to cover them up. This humble tool does, however, have a degree of creative potential that is worth consideration. A rubber can lift out lighter areas from an area of mid-tone (usually made with either charcoal or pencil) to suggest highlights. Alternatively, use the rubber to take the background away: for a drawing that features a dark form against a light backdrop, start dark and draw into it with the rubber to reveal the form. In all cases, you can then return with your pencil or charcoal to reassert the darker tones as you see fit. This process is similar to sculpture, as you're carving out the shapes and tones, rather than adding them in. Drawing with a rubber helps you to rediscover the essential and determine what is worth saving.

There is a wide variety of rubbers available, some more suited to particular functions than others. Putty rubbers are soft and squidgy and respond well when used sensitively. You can either use the edge for broader areas or twist a piece off for more intricate detail. They do tend to get pretty dirty though. Plastic rubbers are much firmer, easier to control and thus ideal for sharp edges. For the crispest line, use a craft knife to cut a small piece off and make sure that the rubber doesn't smudge areas you don't want smudged by rubbing it clean before you use it. Blu-Tack is also good for removing pencil and charcoal, as it lifts unwanted marks without damaging the paper surface.

White pastel or crayon will allow you to draw back into your subject. Using a combination of both darkening and lightening tools can help you explore the full range of tonal values.

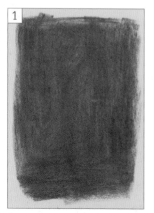

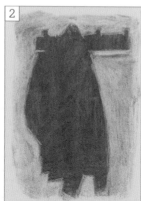

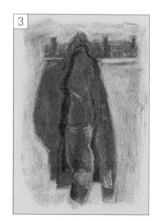

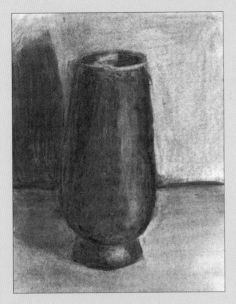

This drawing of a vase started out as a piece of paper blackened with charcoal that was then reworked with a rubber.

Rubbers are inexpensive. Buying a good selection won't break the bank, and will provide you with a few more options when it comes to value drawing. Lay down rough areas of charcoal or pencil and play around with the various lines and techniques.

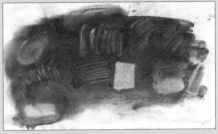

Using different rubbers, indeed different parts of the rubber, will open up a new range of techniques for you to explore.

Using a rubber to draw with can produce some very subtle effects. I just gently stroked some of the graphite away in this drawing of a spoon to suggest the highlights, and that was all that was needed.

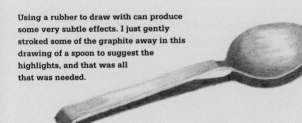

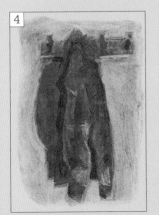

4

5

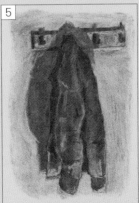

The jacket on a hook appears out of the charcoal base. The form is found initially with an rubber, then worked again with more charcoal. Lastly, some highlights are added with white chalk.

Colour

The range of coloured drawing materials and the effects they provide is so vast that to do them proper justice would require another book. It is worth discussing the fundamentals of colour theory here, and introducing you to a few ideas you might like to explore further.

Colour can add a whole new vibrancy or mood to your drawings, particularly when done well. It makes sense, particularly for the beginner, to take it slowly: don't be tempted to blitz your pictures with a thousand rainbow shades just because you can. As with so many other areas of drawing, less is often more.

The Colour Wheel

Colour theory can be a complex science, but at a basic level, colours are either primary, secondary or tertiary. Red, yellow and blue are primary, as they cannot be made from combinations of any other colours. Secondary colours are products of any two primaries: orange (red and yellow); green (yellow and blue); violet (blue and red). Tertiary colours are those made

by mixing one primary and one secondary (red and orange; red and violet; yellow and orange; yellow and green; blue and green; blue and violet). Neutrals are black, white and grey. Looking at the colour wheel, those that fall opposite one another are known as complementary colours. When placed next to each other, they make the other look brighter, something exploited to great effect in logos and advertising. Mix complementaries together and you get varying shades of brown or grey.

In practice though, colours rarely have such a simple makeup, so it pays to experiment with laying down coloured areas on scrap paper before using them in your drawings. Layer the colours you think you need, adding more layers or increasing the pressure for extra density if

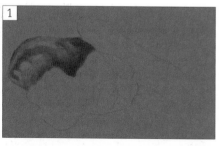

1

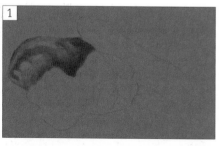

3

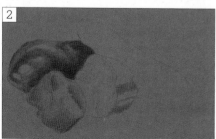

2

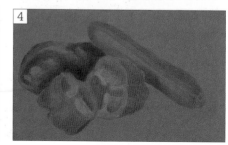

4

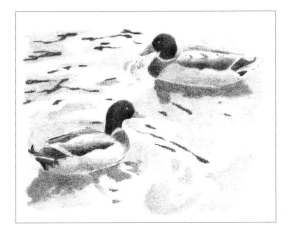

While researching for this book, I found a simple monochrome pencil drawing of two ducks that I had made a few years earlier. It was livened up with green head feathers, yellow bills and feet. I also added a few light touches of blue to the water. The drawing kept its simplicity and calm, while the colour added something extra.

required. You may want to think about using different-coloured paper, which will make your colours brighter and more intense than a plain white surface. Coloured paper also creates an immediate mood before you've even started.

See how the grey card onto which these vegetables were drawn immediately throws them into a sharp relief. The colour is pushed out with a vivid strength.

TRY THIS . . .

Revisit old sketches and drawings by adding colour. You don't need to go overboard with either the number of colours or the amount you lay down. Think about the monochrome composition and tease it out with a few carefully chosen lines or areas of colour. That may be all you need.

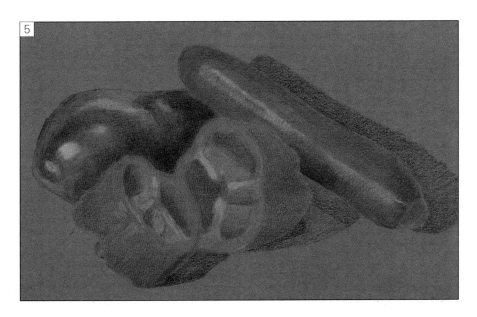

5

Project: Portrait

Having looked at the various ways of using value and colour, it's time to consider combining some of the exercises in a larger composition. The portrait is one of the grand traditions in Western art, and at first may scare the bejeezus out of you. The human face is our portal into the world around us, and often determines our perception of others. It is loaded with subtlety, nuance and significance. To focus on it alone, and more importantly, do it justice, is a challenge. Misjudge just one feature and the rest of the picture could well end up looking like someone else, or just plain odd. You could always adopt the Picasso line; when a viewer remarked that sitter Gertrude Stein did not resemble his portrait of her, he famously replied, 'She will'.

Equipment
- Heavy paper
- Conté crayon
- Toilet tissue
- Rubber
- Fixative spray

Drawing a convincing portrait really does force you to look and look and look. The shapes and arrangement of features on any given head follow a standard genetic formula, yet slight variations are what make us individual. You must therefore notice the interrelation of each form and focus on the shapes and shapes alone.

Finding a model should be pretty easy – ask to sketch a friend or relative while they're watching TV or reading a book, for instance. Make sure they'll be happy sitting still for a period of time, though, and allow them (and yourself) to take regular breaks. And if you can't find a model, grab a decent-size mirror and try drawing yourself. Make sure the room is warm enough and away from any distractions. Consider your lighting setup, which is particularly appropriate here as we're focusing on tone: carefully positioned lamps will cast some interesting shadows on your model's face.

Portraits are often drawn from a three-quarter viewpoint. The head is angled to show its full three-dimensionality, avoiding flattening caused by a straight-on or profile view. Warm yourself up with a few quick sketches (between two and five minutes each) before settling down for the longer pose. Start with light, gentle marks and commit yourself more to the portrait as your confidence grows.

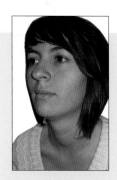

Selecting a Subject
For the project here, my friend Mădălina volunteered to be my subject. I drew a few quick sketches to familiarise myself with her features, then took some photographs. The lighting was kept purposefully soft to reveal the subtle variations in value, and I decided that a bistre-coloured Conté crayon would be a suitable medium. Mădălina's face was angled to the three-quarter view.

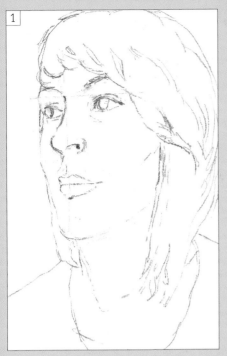

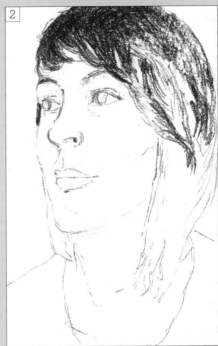

1 To start, I made a rough outline of Mădălina's essential features. Notice how the soft, straight horizontal line across from the top of the left eye and the vertical line leading down the nose were used as marker points. From these features the rest of the face was sketched in.

2 Looking at the face, I assessed where the darkest values were going to be; namely, the upper part of the hair and the eyes. Working on the hair established that base note.

3 The darkest areas of hair were blended slightly, and the rest roughly sketched in, leaving the lightest areas blank. The eyebrows and eyes were then given more detail. The broader side of the crayon was used for drawing in the thicker areas, while the more detailed features, like the eyes, could be worked on with the harder, more precise crayon tip.

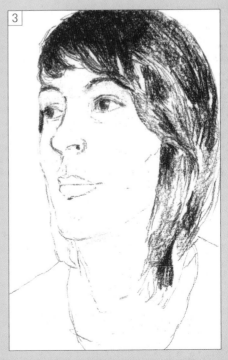

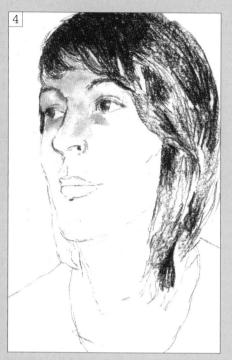

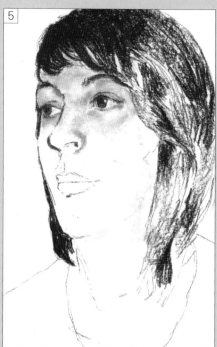

4 I then turned to the skin. Softly working the crayon against the grain of the paper, I laid down shaded areas, then blended them carefully with some small rolled-up sections of toilet tissue.

5 The dark shadow of Mădălina's nose was another area that could be drawn with the harder crayon tip as the face around the eyes was shaded with softer strokes and blended with more tissue.

6 As I continued modelling the face, I tried to keep the crayon as soft as possible and as true to Mădălina's facial structure as I could. How the bowls of her eye sockets and the shape of her nose, for example, would feel informed the portrait. Using Conté is perfect for such pictures as it allows for considerable sensitivity.

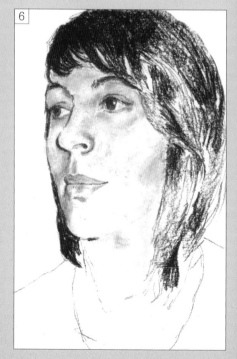

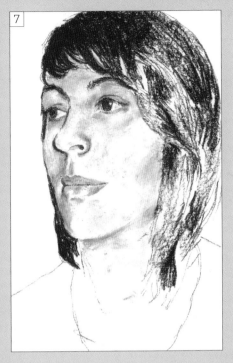

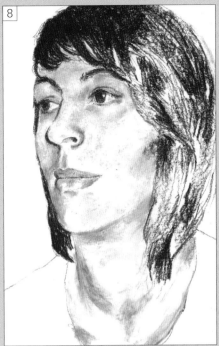

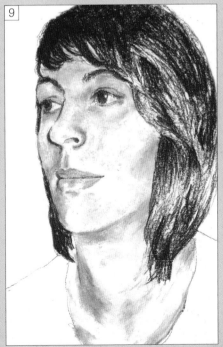

7 The subtle variations of the rest of Mădălina's face were drawn next, including the soft shadows created by her jaw …

8 … and the neck. Remember to always be aware of the structure and the underlying anatomy of your sitter, and take your time to look and notice the interrelationship between the individual parts.

9 Having smoothed out any rough edges with more tissue, I looked again at the hair, suggesting the texture with the hard crayon tip and further shading certain darker areas. I decided to forgo the detail of Mădălina's jumper to focus attention on her face. Finally, any grubby surrounding marks were erased, and the image was sprayed with fixative to seal it.

Surface

Having looked at how line and value can describe the shape of your subject and the play of light upon it, let's focus now on the surface (which in itself is clearly determined by both line and value). What textures you choose to depict add an extra layer to the picture and tell stories about your subject, like the grain of wood, moss on a stone or the details of a feather.

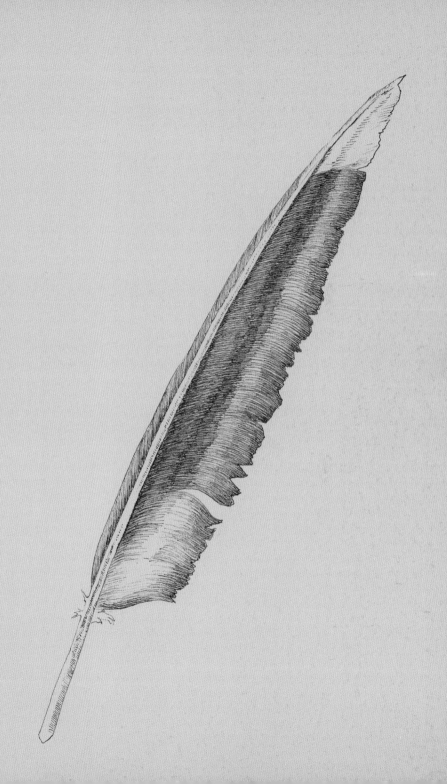

Textures

Hard, soft, airy, serrated, mushy, gnarled, slippery: the physical world is more than just shape and tone – it is tactile, too. Conveying how your subject feels as well as how it looks is a good skill to practise as you encourage your viewer to sympathise and engage more with your final drawings. You should also find that your relationship with each subject deepens as you define it more closely.

Power of the Mind

The ability to accurately convey how something feels has intrigued artists throughout the ages. The rich and powerful garnished with expensive fabrics and jewels; the hardworking farmer with soil under his fingernails; the craggy rocks of a coastline; the serene calm of a glassy lake: they each tell us something about the subject and the artist who depicted it. They are realised as another surface: the surface of the pen or pencil on the page.

One particularly useful way of tackling textures has already been discussed on page 58, when you closed your eyes and felt your subject as you drew. Here, you should keep your eyes open, but it is important to still think about your surfaces even though they are not in your hands. As you draw hair, for example, consider what hair feels like between your fingers. If

you're drawing a crumbling wall, imagine your hands on the bricks and let that information feed into the marks you make. Concentrate too on the drawing material in your hand – the direction and length of each stroke determines the type of texture you convey.

A further step to take is to handle your drawing tool as each different surface dictates. If you're drawing something rough, use your tool roughly: increase the pressure on the paper and be less considered. Similarly, be more gentle and sensitive with your medium if depicting something smooth. Remember though that too much texture can cancel itself out and overload your picture. Pick and choose which surfaces to describe and give them room to breathe. You'll also want to avoid going in too strong – start with lighter areas, then add more if necessary. And above all, stay patient.

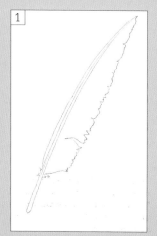

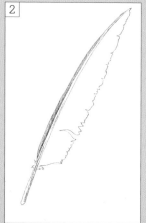

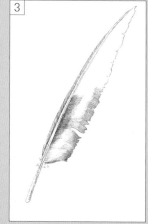

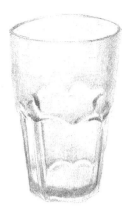

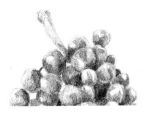

The light bouncing off this bunch of shiny grapes makes them look even more juicy.

It seemed suitable for a glass tumbler to be drawn with a hard grade of pencil to capture its cold reflections.

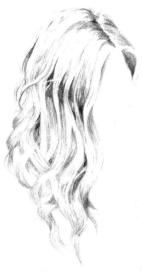

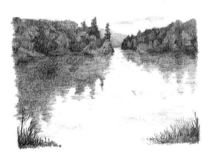

The reflections on this lake were drawn with a fluid tone. I was thinking about the pencil skimming over the surface of the water as I drew.

Hair is notoriously difficult to capture with sufficient life and texture. Concentrate on the play of light around the head as a whole, rather than trying to include each individual strand.

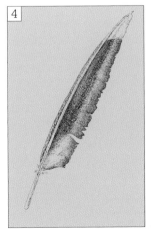

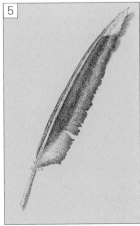

I found this gull's feather in the street. I used the smallest-width fibre-tip pen to gently tease out the details and the feather's fragile strength.

Textures for Textures

You don't just have to rely on your powers of control over each particular medium when it comes to depicting different textures. You can also exploit the very surface you're working on for some interesting results, and similarly, get more hands-on with what you are depicting.

Paper

As mentioned on pages 28–9, paper comes in a variety of thicknesses and finishes, and these can be incorporated into your drawing. Heavier paper may have a grain that you can detect by rubbing your fingertips over it; the deeper troughs in the grain trap the pigment from your drawing tool (ideally charcoal or pastel), and this is true with even the lightest application. So already the surface of your paper is working for you, in terms of creating extra visual interest that you may want to explore.

Rubbings

Children are often encouraged to make rubbings of random objects as a way of connecting a picture with the real world, and vice versa. In the adult world of art historians this has a suitably more grown-up name ('frottage', from the French *frotter*, 'to rub'), yet the appeal remains the same. Rubbings leave a facsimile of your chosen object on the paper – every detail is perfect, yet the object is missing, like a memory or a ghost.

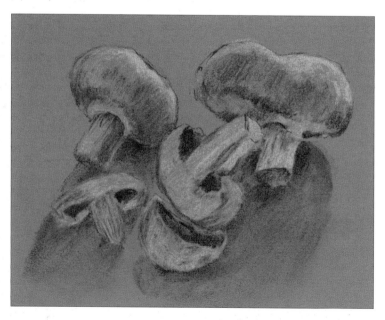

Using a dense, smooth grey paper seemed most appropriate for tackling this group of mushrooms in charcoal. Their dark undersides contrast with the rest of the drawing; while the shadow is drawn with soft, light strokes.

Your paper needs to be quite thin (too thick and you won't pick anything up). Charcoal, pastel, wax crayon or a soft pencil will work best. Choose a hard, textured surface, and bear in mind that even the most mundane objects, such as a wall or paving stone, can yield some interesting effects. You can then draw on top of your rubbings to make a larger composition, or you can tear or cut them up and use the pieces as a basis for a collage. Incorporating the tactile world in your drawings is just one of many ways to reconnect with the pleasure of art-making.

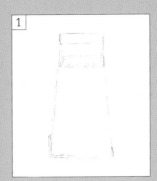
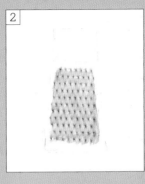
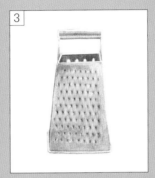
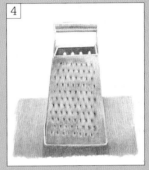
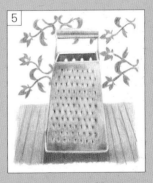

TRY THIS . . .

Wander around your home armed with something to rub onto and something to rub with. Start looking at your surroundings purely in terms of their surfaces. Investigate both large and small areas (a wall and a paper clip, for example), and use different colours too. Label each source, and you'll build up a kind of texture library that you can then dip into when the need arises.

I sketched out the rough shape of the cheese grater, then rubbed its side directly onto the drawing with a soft pencil. The table and background were then added, with the edge of a sketchbook rubbed over the tabletop to add more texture and depth.

Project: Architecture

If you want to get your teeth into texture in the context of a larger composition, you could do no better than to focus on buildings. Whether a tumbledown cottage or a sprawling modernist conurbation, the built environment reveals much about us and the way we live. Furthermore, architecture is rich in surface – brick, concrete, plaster and tarmac all bear witness to the ravages of time, weather and human usage.

Equipment

- Slightly heavy paper
- HB pencil
- Charcoal
- Toilet tissue
- Fixative spray
- Leaves
- Coloured pencils
- Compressed charcoal
- Rubber

Choose your subject carefully, and consider all available viewpoints. Are you going to sit for a few hours working in the open air, or will you make some detailed sketches and/or take a few photographs and work from those? Are there any outside forces that might disrupt the drawing process – will the view get blocked by a car in a driveway, for example? And how will the movement of light affect your picture?

Decide also what textures will work best for you and how you intend to incorporate them into the final drawing, remembering the point, already made, that less is more (overloading a picture with too much information can make it top-heavy, almost suffocating). Remember also that by allowing your drawing room to breathe, the viewer can feel his or her way around it much more easily.

A Local Art Gallery

On a bright fall day, I went for a walk in the local park to gather together a few ideas. I came across an art gallery tucked away among trees and decided that it would make a great subject. I circled the building, taking photographs from a variety of angles and distances. I also picked up a few of the fallen leaves from the surrounding trees to take back to the studio. This picture was chosen to be my starting point – I really liked the play of light and shadow and the scope for playing around with a few different textures too.

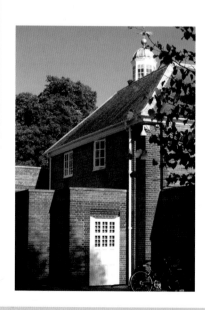

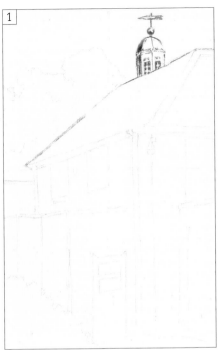

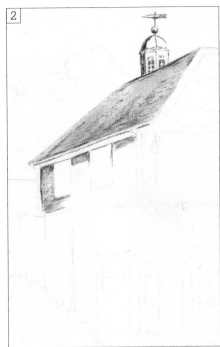

1 I first laid down the bare bones of this picture in pencil. I kept the strokes light to avoid interfering with the charcoal that would be added on top. See how I chose to disregard the bicycle on the right (the detail would have been too difficult and distracting) and added some bushy growth at the bottom left to close off that corner.

2 I continued to add detail in charcoal to the roof and one of the walls, using light strokes and blending it in using the rounded ends of toilet tissue.

3 I then added the windows, as well as some of the texture of the walls. I used a small piece of charcoal, broken off from the main stick, to mark over the shaded areas to suggest the brickwork, and used it more heavily for shaded areas.

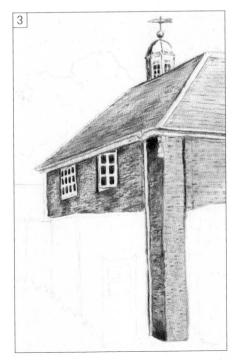

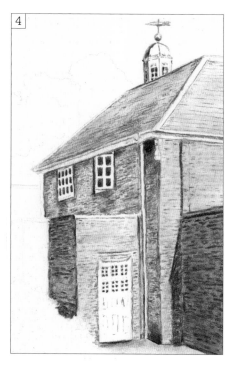

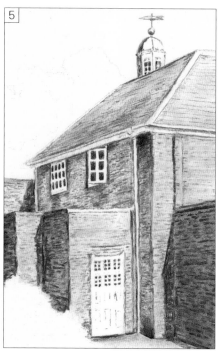

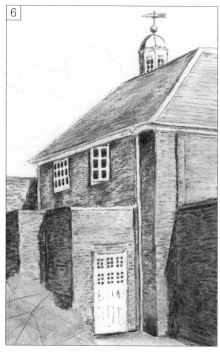

4 I added more walls and more detail. Remember to keep a spare piece of paper under your drawing hand to prevent accidental smudges. You'll want to wash your hands every now and then to keep things clean and tidy.

5 Notice how, as the drawing takes shape, the initial pencil lines don't need to be rubbed out, as the charcoal comfortably occupies the space they once filled.

6 Once I was happy with the appearance of the building, I sealed it with fixative. I could then turn to adding a little more texture and colour. Even though I was using charcoal, I had chosen a paper that would still allow for some leaf rubbings to show through clearly.

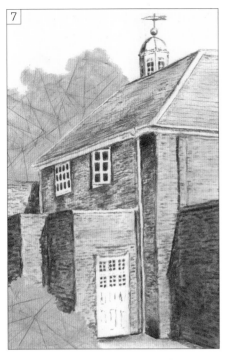

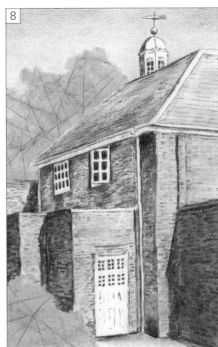

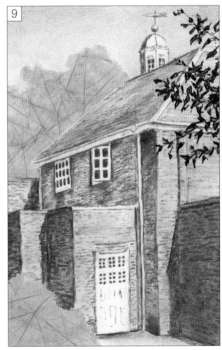

7 Using one or two different leaves at various angles, I rubbed their veins through with a few different shades of green coloured pencil ...

8 ... followed by a light working of blue over the top to try to capture some of that glorious bright, clear autumn sky.

9 As a final point, I used a mixture of compressed charcoal and green coloured pencil to add greater depth to the final drawing by sketching in a few of the branches nearest to the viewer. They weren't drawn precisely; just enough to give some sense of space. After I applied another layer of fixative, the drawing was complete.

Moving On

We've reached the end of the book: has practice made you perfect? It's doubtful, and that's as it should be. Hopefully you have enough to continue on with. Here are a few ideas on where to take your next steps.

Revisiting the Book

Refresh your memory regarding certain subjects by revisiting some of the exercises, maybe even the ones you didn't particularly enjoy the first time around. With newly acquired awareness and skills, your attitude may well have shifted. That said, if you don't enjoy dealing with multi-point perspective, for example, then there is no point forcing it (unless you want to practise being a suffering artist). The idea is to use the exercises and what you've learned as starting points for exploring areas that you find more interesting. It may be obvious, but if there's a specific area you wish to return to, use the index at the back to locate it quickly.

The Loosening Up examples (pages 54–63) are useful for any artist, regardless of level, who finds him or herself up against a wall of apathy or creative staleness. They're quick, easy to get started on, and could just help get the juices flowing again.

Materials

Once you start to feel more comfortable drawing, and your self-confidence travels a few rungs up the ladder, you might want to begin thinking about using different materials. A trip to the local art shop will demonstrate that there is always something else you can try – a new kind of drawing tool, some weird new paper, a rubber that looks interesting. That said, it can also be very useful to stick with what you know, certainly when you are just starting out. It's also a lot cheaper. Be aware of what is available and certainly invest in things that are worthwhile: just be wary of buying something because it looks like the kind of thing you ought to buy, rather than something you know you're going to actually use and enjoy.

You may also want to try using materials not really mentioned in this book so far. Painting, animation, film, printmaking, even sculpture (a kind of drawing in space) are all there to be investigated and enjoyed.

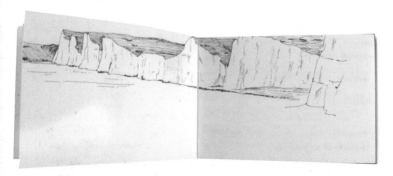

A small sketchbook allows you to record moments of inspiration and interest. Think of it as a visual diary, and keep it with you always.

Mixing Things Up

Although this book has been divided into separate sections, you can of course investigate what happens when you bring together two or more: perspective and surface; value and line; perspective, surface, value and line. Indeed, many drawings you go on to make will and should incorporate different elements: this will become more natural as your skills improve.

As already mentioned, drawing is not photography, and editing and re-editing your compositions will hone your creative eye. If an object is crowding your layout, or even if you just don't fancy drawing it, leave it out. Likewise, include elements from other sources to bolster the drawing's final appeal. Remember to think about the light source and drawing style so you can integrate these additions successfully.

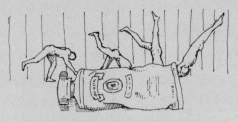

This collage of two very different things has led to an intriguing, strange drawing. The tube of oil paint and the figure-in-motion studies – what can it all mean?

Rules

Rules are made to be broken – never was a truer word said. Art is such a subjective pursuit, and it's impossible to say to someone that the way they are doing it is 'wrong'. The drills in this book have been designed to equip you in the basics of a practice that is centuries old. But essential to a successful artistic practice, on whatever level, is curiosity. It keeps you hungry and keeps you looking, and a certain inquisitiveness will do you no harm. What happens when you reverse the rules of aerial perspective, making things in the distance crystal clear while blurring everything in the foreground? Are your marks more interesting if you continually draw, then erase, draw, then erase, the same subject on the same piece of paper? Take yourself out of the comfort zone, if only to remind yourself how nice and comfortable it was in the first place.

Look Around

Drawing is a way of engaging with our surroundings. Stay alert and keep a small sketchbook with you at all times. Jot down quick sketches, notes and ideas. Take photos with your mobile phone. Cut out pictures from magazines and newspapers. Take screen grabs from Internet pages you find exciting. Let your eyes drink in shapes, colours, textures, lines and other moments of visual and mental pleasure. As someone who draws, you are now part of a

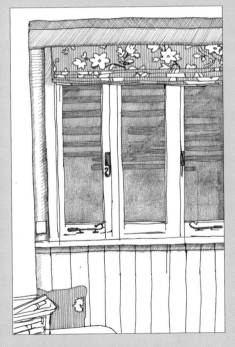

This drawing mixes pen, pencil and coloured pencils. Some of the lines were kept purposely flat to contrast with the receding ceiling beams reflected in the window.

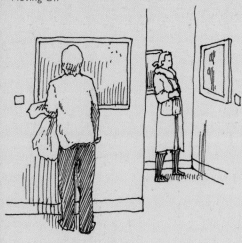

Join the artistic fraternity. Visit galleries and museums for both temporary exhibitions and displays from the permanent collections.

with your drawing. Think about friends or family members, places that you find visually exciting, or locations that hold good memories.

You may find that your areas of personal interest have already been visited by previous artists. If you're into technology, for example, look at the Futurists (active in the early 20th century, they were obsessed with the aesthetic impact of the dawning age of the machine); if you're a political animal, consider the work of the Russian Constructivists or Mexicans Diego Rivera and Frida Kahlo. Seeing the directions that past artists have taken their passions can open up new areas to discover. Furthermore, as you look at more art, your own personal taste will be honed and refined. Finding artists that you like, for whatever reason, will take you further into their work, cement your interest and lead to new discoveries.

rich heritage. Be guided by the footsteps of those who walked the path before you, and learn from them. Galleries, museums, libraries, bookshops and the Internet are filled with resource material for you to sink your teeth into. Visiting large gallery collections can be daunting with so much to see. Allow your instinct to pick and choose, almost at random, what takes your particular fancy, or do some homework beforehand and focus on particular rooms of interest. Your sketchbook will be a perfect companion for such trips, enabling you to record moments of inspiration and delight.

Get Personal

Finding and drawing subjects that have a personal relevance will enrich the working process. Rolling landscapes and vases of flowers have their place, of course, but if you don't feel inspired or interested, then no amount of toiling at the paper surface will reward you. Subjects such as things from your childhood or items that you use every day, for example, may very well motivate you to engage fully

Classes

Art is for the large part a solitary activity, and you may get to a point where you need some inspiration or input from other people. Search the Internet for art groups in your area or visit the local library or art shops, where you may find posters or leaflets. Classes offer an informal opportunity for people with similar interests and wildly different abilities to meet, work together and discuss art. Talking about your work can help you progress, as it forces you to take a step back and reflect on what you're doing. Classes may be led by a tutor or not – the structure and dynamics will vary. Don't be

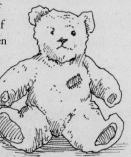

Subjects like old childhood toys, especially the well-loved ones, may make you respond to the drawing process with a new sensitivity.

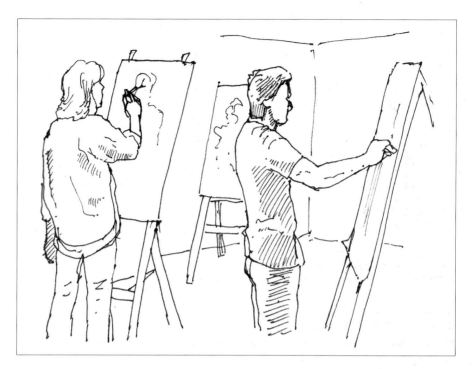

A well-organised art class can foster a real sense of confidence in your own work. Your fellow students will also share similar interests despite very different backgrounds.

too intimidated on your first visit – everyone has to start at some point. If you can't find anything local, how about setting a class up yourself?

Competitions

Details of these can again be found online or in the back of specialty magazines. Entering competitions is normally pretty cheap, and can help you step up to the mark and improve yourself. Prizes range from paltry to impressive and most relate to artistic endeavour. And there's nothing like a deadline to focus your mind and force you into work mode.

The Perfect Artist

Keep looking and keep drawing. By doing this, you'll find that your notion of what 'perfect' actually means will shift and evolve accordingly. You'll start to look at things in a different light. You'll scrutinise things more rigorously. You'll engage more with the world around you.

Art never has an end point. The more we do, the more we discover; the more we discover, the more we realise how little we know. It is a constant learning process. Remember all you learned here, or at least some of it – the things you found most rewarding. Cherish your pictures. Some that once felt spot-on will seem almost embarrassingly naïve a few years later. Others will, however, always hit the mark. Keep hold of them, as they all map this path you're now on – your own personal journey as a continually practising, continually perfecting drawing artist.

Tips and Hints

This book is a compendium of tips and hints on how to improve your drawing skills. Here, some of the most essential points have been broken down and presented in easily digestible chunks for your drawing pleasure. They can be referred to time and again, and will always be relevant, no matter what stage you are at.

Materials

• Break individual pieces of charcoal off from the main stick. Because it's such a fragile medium, smaller bits are easier to control.

• To sharpen charcoal, hold a piece of very fine sandpaper with one hand, and with the other firmly rub the end of the charcoal, held at an angle, to get a neat chisel tip. Don't press too hard or the stick will snap.

• Remember that pencils come in a variety of grades. For a drawing with full tonal range, use at least two different grades.

• A piece of scrap paper should be as important to you as your other media. Use it to test out your tools and clean rubber edges. Keep a fresh piece of paper under your drawing hand so you don't smudge the work you've already done.

• Particularly at the start, limit yourself to a well-chosen but small range of materials. Stick with a few items rather than overloading yourself and your wallet.

• Your choice of material will determine the extent of the techniques available to you. If you want to draw a particularly atmospheric tone drawing, for example, then don't reach for the felt-tip pens. Get familiar with how each material behaves, feels and looks, and choose accordingly.

Smaller pieces of charcoal snapped from the main stick are easier to handle.

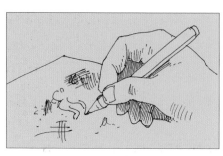

A piece of scrap paper can be used to try out materials and clean dirty ones.

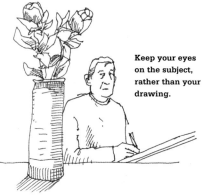

Keep your eyes on the subject, rather than your drawing.

Process

• Don't run before you can walk. Take your time with each part of the drawing process, and allow your confidence to grow. Don't pressure yourself too much by expecting greatness from day one.

• Each of the exercises in this book is about the process rather than the final picture.

• Draw what you see, rather than what you know to be there. The mind can play funny tricks with the artist's eye. It might help to think of an unrelated object that your subject resembles. A classic example is likening the human body to a rolling landscape. This helps you dissociate yourself from any connections you may have to your subject, conscious or otherwise, and focuses you on just looking.

• Avoid drawing in full light, as it can strain your eyes.

• As a musician continually practises scales, arpeggios and other smaller exercises, keep practising the drills in this book to keep your eye-to-hand coordination fresh and supple. You could also invent one or two exercises of your own.

• Keep your work area clean and free of clutter. You may want to put down some newspaper before starting, particularly if you're using materials like charcoal and pastel.

• Keep your eyes moving, but focus primarily on your subject rather than your drawing. The more you see, the more you will draw.

• Breaking your subject down into its constituent parts (lines, curves and angles) should help your drawing method no end. Approach it as if you've never seen it before.

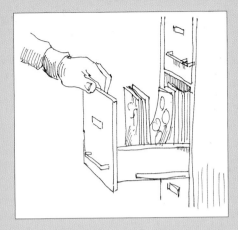

Keep your drawings stored somewhere clean, where they can be easily accessed at a later date.

• Start by drawing your subject with light lines and minimal pressure. This way any mistakes can be rectified without damaging the paper.

• Look at your drawing upside down or reflected in a mirror to check for accuracy – you could be surprised at what it reveals.

• Once your drawing is finished, put it away for a week or two, then have another look at it. It pays to revisit old work with a fresh pair of eyes – your attitude towards it may change, you may see room for improvement, or like bits that you previously weren't happy with. Develop a critical mind (but not overly so).

• Stick with your drawing, even if it's not going well. Reserve your judgement for the end.

• Start with simple subjects that you can draw confidently, then move on to more complex and challenging ones.

• Keep all your drawings – looking back on them after a while will reveal how much progress you're making.

Glossary

Aerial/atmospheric perspective
The means of creating a convincing sense of distance by observing atmospheric effects. Thus, objects in the background are less detailed, colours are weaker and cooler, and values have less contrast.

Aerial/bird's-eye view
Observing from a high elevation; i.e., looking down on an object or scene.

Asymmetrical
A design or form that, when divided along its central axis, is unevenly balanced.

Axis
An implied or visible straight line that suggests movement or gives structure.

Blending
The merging of one colour or value into another. Best achieved with softer drawing materials.

Blind contour
A line drawing made without looking at the paper. Good for exercising hand-eye coordination.

Cast shadow
The shadow formed by an object in the direction away from the light source.

Chiaroscuro
The interplay of light and dark, and a means of increasing the illusion of space. Particularly important for artists of the Renaissance.

Composition
The arrangement and balance of various elements into a harmonious picture.

Contour
The outline of different elements.

Contrast
The relationship between two separate elements within the same composition.

Cross-hatching
The buildup of a series of parallel lines, drawn at different angles, to create areas of various values.

Eye level
Your line of vision in relation to your subject; in other words, your own imaginary or drawn horizon. Also known as the horizon-line.

Focal point
The primary feature (or features) within a composition, usually drawn with greater detail and contrast.

Foreshortening
The effect of perspective within a single object. Elements nearest the viewer appear larger and get smaller as they recede.

Gesture
A spontaneous, instinctive means of conveying form, with the focus on movement.

Golden Section
A mathematical system of proportion in which focal points appear approximately $5/13$ of the way across.

Grid
A lattice of criss-crossed or parallel lines. Also a method of dividing a drawing into smaller parts to help in composition or enlarging.

Highlight
The lightest part of a drawing.

Landscape
A drawing of an outside scene, usually open countryside. Also refers to the format in which the paper's horizontal length is greater than its vertical length.

Leading line
A drawn or suggested line that leads the eye into the composition.

Mark
A line, a dot, a scratch – anything that leaves a visible impression on the drawing surface.

Mass
An object's weight or density.

Medium
Any drawing tool (plural media).

Multipoint
An object receding upwards or downwards in space in relation to eye level.

Negative space
The space surrounding an object.

One-point perspective
All receding parallels converge into one central point at eye level.

Overworking
Revisiting a drawing and adding more line or value in a different medium or technique.

Perspective
A system for depicting spatial depth, with objects getting smaller the further away they are (see also 'one-point perspective' and 'two-point perspective').

Picture plane
The flat, two-dimensional surface you draw on.

Proportion
The relationship of one element to another within a drawing, and their relationship to the picture as a whole.

Representational/figurative drawing
A form of drawing that gets close to the actual appearance of a subject and strives for a sense of realism.

Shading
Creating areas of light and dark to suggest space and depth.

Sighting
The process of measuring objects and the spaces between them.

Subject
The main theme or object being depicted.

Texture
The surface quality of a shape or volume.

Two-point perspective
Receding parallels converging into two points on the horizon; one left and the other right.

Value
The range of light and dark tones: usually black, white and all greys in between.

Vanishing point
The point in perspective at which receding parallel lines appear to converge.

Volume
The overall shape and bulk of an object.

Index

About the Author

Matt Pagett is a London-based writer, illustrator and artist. He has exhibited his work internationally, including a solo show at Miscelanea gallery in Barcelona, Spain. He has authored and illustrated numerous books, including *This Is Not a Book, 101 Golden Rules of Fishing* and *The Best Dance Moves in the World…Ever!* Images from the latter were developed and used extensively throughout an exhibition about dance at The Lowry in Manchester, England.

He has an MA in Art History from Edinburgh University, and is currently studying for an MA in Printmaking at the Royal College of Art, London.

Drawing has always been at the heart of Matt's artistic output. He has used a variety of methods and media, from the traditional to the digital, and he continues to explore the various ways in which drawing can inform how we look at and relate to the world around us.

Examples of his work can be seen at **www.mattpagett.co.uk**

Image Credits

All images © Quid Publishing with the exception of the following:

15   Cave painting, Lascaux, France
      Public Domain

15   *Praying Hands*, Dürer
      Public Domain

15   *Simeon and Jesus in the Temple*, Rembrandt
      © David Lees | Corbis

15   *Roman Ruins*, Canaletto
      © Geoffrey Clements | Corbis

15   *Men and Women Dancing*, Hokusai
      © Asian Art & Archaeology, Inc. | Corbis

15   *Fishing Boats on the Beach at Maries-de-la-Mer*, Van Gogh
      © Christie's Images/CORBIS

16   Map of the Planets
      © Kuko | Dreamstime

16   Old Street Map of New York City
      © Tektite | Dreamstime

16   Architectural Blueprint
      © Lookaround | Dreamstime

17   Peace Sign
      Public Domain

17   *Let Sam Do It*, Winsor McCay
      © Bettmann | Corbis

17   U.S. Political Symbols
      © Cheryl Graham | iStockphoto

17   Beanpod Botanical Illustration
      Public Domain

96   Study of the head of Saint Anne
      Public Domain